Self-Discipline in 10 days

How To Go From Thinking To Doing

by
Theodore Bryant, MSW

HUB Publishing
Human Understanding and Behavior Publishing
Seattle, Washington

Self-Discipline in 10 days

Copyright © 2003

ISBN: 1-880115-02-6

Library of Congress Catalog Card Number: 98-75039

Printed in the United States of America

Dedicated . . .

to all the people who have attended my self-discipline courses, seminars, and lectures. You provided me with the desire and motivation to write this book. You enabled me to create a self-discipline system that can work for anyone. But, more important, you taught me that life's greatest pleasure lies in helping others accomplish their desires. For this simple lesson, I thank you from the bottom of my heart.

Table Of Contents

Table Of Contents

Part Three
Subconscious Beliefs plus Five Power Tools

Part Four
Putting It All Together

Part One

Preliminary Information

Important!

Whenever and wherever I conduct self-discipline workshops, seminars, or classes, I always hear this question: "Can I actually improve my self-discipline in only ten days?"

My answer:

YES...YES...YES

Absolutely. Positively. Definitely. Actually, you will experience improvement in one day! Your improvement will be in direct proportion to how closely you follow the program in this book. A partial effort will generate a partial result.

The exercises, tips, and techniques contained in this book came from many different and diverse sources. This book contains the quickest and easiest methods currently available for improving self-discipline. Did you notice that I did not say "The best methods"? The *best* methods can take lots of time and tons of effort to understand and employ. In this book you will find methods that will work fast and painless; we will use a no-frills approach. But I promise that you will learn more than you will need to improve your self-discipline immediately. To facilitate your consumption and digestion of this material, all psychobabble and jargon have been skimmed off. So you're getting only the real goods in a powerful and concentrated dose.

Trust me. The system in this book will give you the insight, techniques, and tips to quickly improve your self-discipline skill. You will note that I said, "skill." That is because my experiences with thousands of people have taught me that self-discipline is simply a skill that anyone can learn to use. No one comes into the world with it. And improving self-discipline, like improving any skill, is simply a matter of education and practice.

Some of us learned self-discipline from parents, friends, or relatives. Others of us learned it through school, sports, the armed forces, or maybe even through our own intuition. Unfortunately, however, most of us were never taught the psychology of self-discipline, how it really works. So we can't always use it when we need it. This book will help you learn what you need to know, and unlearn what you need to drop. Soon you will be aware of many tools, techniques, and concepts to help you unravel the mystery of self-discipline. You are going to be amazed at how quickly and easily this self-discipline system works. Sound promising? Then let's get started.

Read this ☞

How to use this guidebook

First, you'll jump into the chapter titled, *Preliminary Information*. This section is filled with information that will put your whole self to work for you. Before you tackle the ten-day self-discipline plan, be sure that you are familiar with all the information in the *Preliminary Information* chapter. Most self-discipline failures occur because of a lack of psychological preparation. The *Preliminary Information* chapter is designed to provide you with the necessary psychological preparation to make this system work.

Next comes the ten-day program for the development of awareness and attitude. Then, in the *Putting It All Together* section, you'll go into Action. This system evolved over years of experimentation and research. Through classes, workshops, and seminars, I've taught this system to people from all walks of life. Its overall design has a purpose. Each exercise, technique, and lesson was designed to follow the one that precedes it.

"One day at a time" is good advice when making a behavior change. Do not devour this book all at once. Do not skip around from chapter to chapter. While you *don't have to complete the ten-day section in ten consecutive days*, don't spread it out too much. Such an approach, while yielding some benefits, will leave you with the hole rather than the donut. In other words, don't work against yourself.

Prepare yourself for the ten-day program by thoroughly learning the *Preliminary Information*. Then the ten-day portion of the program will zoom past and you'll soon be putting self-discipline into motion. I've seen it happen time and time again. So remember:

Follow the instructions!
Do the exercises in order!

READY?

1.
Getting Started

Caution!

Before you take another step,
meet your greatest obstacle to self-discipline:

Meet Hyde

Every psychological theory recognizes that we are made up of several different selves. So, obviously, we have more than one side of ourselves with which to contend. Moreover, difficulty arises when we consider that frequently our different sides want to go in different directions. Inner conflict, it's called.

Sometimes one side of us wants to engage in a productive activity such as working on a report for work, cleaning the kitchen, or balancing the checkbook. But another side of us wants to watch television and eat chocolate chip cookies, or anything else to avoid doing something we consider a productive use of time. In other words, *there is a part of you that does not want self-discipline.* This side of you we'll call Hyde.

In Robert Lewis Stevenson's classic novel, Dr. Jekyll and Mr. Hyde, we find a literary example that perfectly suits ours needs here. Basically the story is about a benevolent doctor who, through chemical experimentation on himself, brought out the evil side of his personality while suppressing the good side. The two sides of himself ended up in a struggle for dominance that eventually destroyed them both. Think of the part of you that wants self-discipline as Dr. Jekyll, and the part of you that fights your attempts at self-discipline as Hyde. Get the idea? Do not, however, think of your Hyde side as an enemy. Think, instead, of Hyde as the part of you that is creative, fun-loving, and pleasure-seeking; the child side of yourself. You do not want to do battle with Hyde, but you want to recruit Hyde as a partner who supports your self-discipline efforts.

This Jekyll/Hyde approach is one of the more important concepts to understand in your attempts to develop self-discipline. Time and time again, participants in my workshops, seminars, and courses have reaffirmed that this concept, understanding it and applying it, has been instrumental in their self-discipline successes. So, you will begin by learning about how your personal Hyde operates.

Hyde believes:

If I begin a structured, organized journey toward any chosen goal:

☛ *I'll become a slave to routine*

☛ *I'll lose my freedom*

☛ *I'll lose my sense of fun*

☛ *I'll drown in a sea of responsibilities*

☛ *I'll put too much pressure on myself*

We all have a rebellious side to our personalities that resists any form of structure. We bring this rebellious seed from our childhood. One of the first words a child learns to say emphatically is "NO." The child we once were still lives inside us, and every child battles authority. Hyde, the name we will call your inner childlike rebel, battles any form of authority, even if the authority is you. Hyde subconsciously says: "Nobody can tell me what to do, not even me."

You will soon learn how your personal Hyde operates to sabotage your self-discipline efforts. You will also learn how to counteract this self-inflicted negative influence. But beware, you will experience resistance each step of the way from Hyde. In fact, because I consider your understanding of Hyde so important, the first thing we're going to do is learn how Hyde will try to block your efforts at implementing the system laid out in this book.

On your voyage toward developing self-discipline, you'll encounter torpedoes from several sources outside yourself, but your most difficult opposition will come from within. Indeed, in your efforts to develop self-discipline, initially you will be your own worst enemy.

 Remember:
A part of you does not want self-discipline.

We all have a Hyde side: the rebellious, comfort-seeking, non-ambitious part of our personality. This is a condition of being human. So let this serve as a word of warning. Do not allow Hyde to block your efforts.

You'll soon have the know-how necessary to transform Hyde from a pesky saboteur into a loyal assistant. In doing so, you will be doubling the inner resources you need for self-discipline. And, most important, you will *enjoy* self-discipline, rather than experience it as a constant struggle against yourself.

As we've already established, we're going to call the part of you that does not want self-discipline *"Hyde."*

Hyde not only knows all your weaknesses, fears, and insecurities, but also knows how to use them against you. This devious little imp inside you plans to employ every method of manipulation available to keep you from following the program laid out in this book. Why?

Hyde knows that once you develop self-discipline, you'll be your own boss. That means curtains for Hyde's reign. You'll no longer be a slave to the self-defeating traits that keep you from transforming your desires and ideas into actions and accomplishments.

Rest assured that Hyde will childishly resist cooperation. So, your best strategy is to familiarize yourself with Hyde's tactics, most of which operate on a subconscious level, where you are not aware of them. But by familiarizing yourself with Hyde's method of operation, you will soon have Hyde working with you rather than against you.

The next chapter deals with
Hyde's five favorite techniques
for poisoning your efforts.
Even though all of these brands of
poison share certain ingredients,
you'll be wise to consider each
separately. This way you'll be less
susceptible to any of them.

2.
Poisons
&
Antidotes

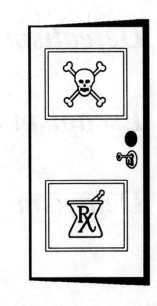

Hyde's five favorite poisons:

❶ *Cynicism*

❷ *Negativism*

❸ *Defeatism*

❹ *Escapism*

❺ *Delayism*

 and their antidotes . . .

❶ *Cynicism*

A cynical person is inclined to question the goodness and value of everything. And because nothing in life is perfect, the cynic can always find a flaw in absolutely anything. Once found, the flaw is then magnified until it overshadows everything else. The cynic is a genius at pointing out why a particular plan, idea, or choice is no good and won't work.

The external cynics such as sarcastic friends, pessimistic relatives, and loser co-workers who delight in finding flaws, can be avoided when you realize that their cynicism is contagious. But Hyde, the inner cynic, goes everywhere with you. So, you will hear whispers from within: "You can't learn self-discipline from a book." "What has this exercise got to do with self-discipline? Why not skip it?" "All this self-help stuff is a lot of fluff." Beware of Hyde.

 Remember:
A part of you does not want self-discipline.

Hyde is a master cynic. Expect that your efforts at implementing this self-discipline system will be constantly bombarded with cynicism from within. "It's too complicated." "It's too easy to have any real value." "It's too difficult to complete." " Blah, blah, blah."

Antidote to Cynicism:

Have faith in your ability to improve. This guidebook will lead you to *improved* self-discipline. Perfection? Of course not. Neither you nor this guidebook is perfect. It would, therefore, be ridiculous to expect perfection. But it would be even more ridiculous to reject all this book's benefits, benefits you can reap by following the system in this book.

If you lock onto the imperfections, then you've allowed Hyde to dupe you. If, however, you cling onto the belief that your powers of self-discipline will substantially improve if you follow the instructions in this program, then you will join the many persons who have discovered the joy of seeing their desires transformed into reality. So when Hyde tries to convince you that this system is a waste of time, be assertive, and respond to Hyde immediately by telling yourself, "If I am now consciously aware of my self-defeating chatter, then *the system is already working!*"

Accomplishment-oriented, present-tense, concrete self-talk is your first line of defense against Hyde's efforts to keep you tied to your old ways. You'll feel a surge of strength the very first time you challenge the Hyde side of yourself.

❷ *Negativism*

It has been said that "If you could give the person who is responsible for most of you troubles a kick in the caboose, you wouldn't be able to sit down for a month." Whoever made this statement must have known about Hyde.

During your initial attempts to improve your self-discipline, you will need to maintain a positive attitude. So guess what? One of Hyde's favorite self-discipline sabotage tactics is to spotlight all of the negative happenings in your life. As you begin to devise goals and plans, Hyde will attempt to direct your attention toward everything unpleasant about the persons, places and things that make up your environment. When Hyde uses this strategy to divert you from your self-discipline improvement program, you'll find yourself saying things like, "Why bother?"

Sure, "Why bother?" After all, your boss is a jerk. Your mate is a turkey. Your shoes are too tight, and so is your underwear. Then there is the polluted state of the environment. There is the constant threat of a war. There are cancer-causing food additives in everything you eat. The planet is dying. The Governor is a sap. Indeed, life is tough and then you die.

So, why should you waste your time, what precious little there is left of it, doing dumb self-discipline exercises? If you cannot think of an answer to that question, then Hyde has got you by the *attitude*. And once that happens, then Hyde's

Negativism   continued...

work is half done because your brain will search for reasons to support negative attitudes. That's the way the brain works. Whatever you tell yourself, negative or positive, your subconscious believes. Your subconscious mind does not weigh evidence and then evaluate your claim. It simply believes what you tell it. Moreover, your subconscious finds reasons to prove you are right, even if you are wrong. Then your subconscious begins to tailor your attitude and behavior to whatever you have told it.

So, in essence, *you create your attitude and behavior by what you tell yourself.* Tell yourself that this self-discipline program will not work and, guess what, it will not work. What a surprise, huh?

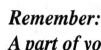

Remember:
A part of you does not want self-discipline.

Antidote to Negativism:

Believe that your *attitude* has everything to do with your success, regardless of the task at hand. Believe that there is just as much good stuff in the world as there is bad stuff.

You decide upon which stuff to focus. That proverbial glass of water that contains fifty percent of its capacity is either half full or half empty, *depending on your attitude.* And you create your own attitude, and your attitude influences your behavior. Always be aware that you have the power to choose a positive attitude. And a positive attitude is your strongest possible antidote to Hyde's tactic of negativism.

Remember: Hyde wants to keep you from multiplying your powers of self-discipline. If that can be accomplished by dampening your spirit, Hyde will do so by reminding you of all that's wrong with the world. On the surface, a negative attitude doesn't seem connected to self-discipline, but rest assured that your overall attitude about life is what steers and fuels your actions. So when you feel yourself (Hyde) using negativity to turn you away from positive action, don't be tricked. Remember: *You can choose your own attitude.* Will your attitude work for you or against you? The choice is yours. Believe it.

❸ *Defeatism*

Cynicism and negativism got married and had a baby. They named it Defeatism. Groucho Marx must have known their kid.

When Groucho was invited to join a hoity-toity Hollywood country club he replied, "I'm not interested in joining any organization that would have me as a member." Funnyman Marx spouted this self-deprecating line for a laugh, but Hyde will try to instill this attitude in you as a roadblock between you and your attempts to implement the system laid out in this guidebook.

Using defeatism, Hyde will try to con you into saying things like: "Maybe this self-discipline program is good, but it probably won't work for *me*." "*I'm* not smart enough to understand this stuff." "*I'm* too smart to be helped by this lame stuff." "*I'm* too old." "*I'm* too young." In other words, Hyde will try to convince you that *the fault lies within you personally*; that *you* somehow lack the ability to turn this system into a reality.

Hyde will attempt to drown your enthusiasm by pointing out all your *perceived* shortcomings, then use them to trick you into self-defeat. Hyde will use any perceived inadequacy to dredge up feelings of insecurity and low self-esteem which will, of course, lead to your either giving up on the system (in reality giving up on yourself), or going about it so halfheartedly that all benefits will be minimized.

Defeatism *continued...*

Even though your intellect will tell you that lots of people have prospered by using the techniques in this book, Hyde will say: "But *you're* different." Then Hyde will furnish a reason (or maybe a hundred reasons) that foster a why-I-won't-succeed attitude. Yes, Hyde will latch onto a personality trait, a physical characteristic, or any other irrelevant quality available, including your race, sex, or religion and turn it into a tool for self-defeat.

Remember:
A part of you does not want self-discipline.

Antidote to Defeatism:

Believe in your ability to profit from knowledge. Believe that the ideas in this self-discipline book will work for you. Some of them have been around for centuries, others come from recently developed psychological approaches to self-management. The tools, tips, and techniques in this book have worked for thousands upon thousands of people, all types of people.

So, when Hyde starts to yap about a trait of yours that will prove insurmountable as you work your way toward improved self-discipline, counter by saying: "Nothing is going to stop me." In other words, don't lament over your shortcomings, redouble your efforts. A belief in yourself, coupled with self-discipline (which you'll soon have, if you don't allow Hyde to cheat you out of it) is a winning combination, regardless of the enterprise you're undertaking. Believe it.

④ *Escapism*

Developing self-discipline requires self-knowledge. Self-knowledge, in turn, requires that you occasionally engage in self-examination, an activity that sometimes evokes anxiety. Like a buried treasure, self-knowledge requires that you dig deep before you can reap the bounty. Inevitably you'll encounter stones during the dig.

Emotional stones, buried in your subconscious, include many events and situations that you'd just as soon leave buried. Unfortunately, however, those stones contain the keys to why certain parts of you refuse to cooperate in your self-discipline efforts. This applies whether you are dieting, running a business, or maintaining an exercise program.

Because being aware of these anxiety-provoking stones is so important in developing self-discipline, some of the exercises in this guidebook require that you unearth and deal with a few stones. Naturally you'll experience some discomfort. Enter Hyde.

Hyde will say: "You don't need to do all that psychological stuff. What do these exercises have to do with learning to organize your time?" "Let's skip actually doing the exercise part, and just read the exercises and think about them. Sure, that'll be enough. Better yet," Hyde will go on to say, "why not go eat that slice of pie in the fridge? Or make a phone call? Television! Of course, that's the ticket. On the Public Broadcasting Network they're showing a swell documentary about horseshoes!" In other words, Hyde will point out other "important" tasks that immediately should be taken care of, anything rather than doing your self-discipline exercises.

Escapism   *continued . . .*

In short, Hyde will try to divert you from the day's exercise, especially if the exercise in question involves any sort of self-examination. Hyde will coax you toward another activity that will instead provide some sort of escape. And because you haven't yet developed the self-discipline that you'll soon have, Hyde uses escapism masterfully. Chances are that you previously have used escapism to dash your efforts at reaching your goals. So, you'll soon learn that Hyde is quite good at employing this method of self-defeat.

Remember:
A part of you does not want self-discipline.

Antidote to Escapism:

Believe that life, for the most part, is based on the cause-and-effect principle. In your life, your actions are the cause; the results of your actions are the effects. Granted, the action you take regarding the self-discovery exercises in this guidebook might occasionally cause you discomfort. But that discomfort will quickly transform into a wonderful feeling of accomplishment as you experience the successes that result from your newly acquired self-knowledge. These successes will *continue throughout your lifetime.*

So when you find yourself attempting to escape the discomfort of self-examination by pursuing a diversionary activity, when Hyde tries to sucker you into escapism by dangling a carrot before you, ask "Is this just a tactic to sway me from my path to self-discipline?"

Remember: The proverbial carrot dangling on the stick is chased by a donkey, often referred to as an ass. Don't let Hyde make one out of you.

❺ *Delayism*

"I'll do it later," is one of Hyde's favorite sentences. Often one of the previously described tactics will be used as the reason to "do it later." Other times a piggyback reason is offered: "I can't begin a weight-loss program *until* I buy a decent outfit to work out in." Hyde has then succeeded in putting a hurdle between you and your goal.

Then Hyde says, "And I can't afford to buy a new outfit *until* I have lowered the balance on my credit cards." Yet another hurdle. On and on it goes until you are completely immobilized by the hurdles between you and your original goal.

Another delay tactic is "I just don't have time." Well, we all have twenty-four hours per day; no more, no less. This holds true regardless of whether you are the head of a nation or the head of a household, or both. "But some of us have more responsibilities than others," Hyde says. True enough, but now we're talking about priorities. What you *choose* to do with your twenty-four hours per day is another matter altogether. And one of the things you have chosen to do is acquire self-discipline.

Remember:
A part of you does not want self-discipline.

Antidote to Delayism:

The point here is to recognize whether a given delay is legitimate; that is to say whether the delay is working for you or against you. This question must be constantly addressed if Hyde's tactic of *delayism* is to be neutralized. Delayism, sometimes in combination with the previously described tactics, will be used to prevent you from doing the exercises suggested in this guidebook.

Remember: Tell yourself that the program can succeed only if the exercises are actually completed, not just thought about. Besides, once you begin using your new knowledge about self-discipline, you'll actually enjoy doing things on time rather than delaying. Believe it.

Summary

Hyde's Five Favorite Poisons:

❶ *Cynicism*

❷ *Negativism*

❸ *Defeatism*

❹ *Escapism*

❺ *Delayism*

Now that you can recognize Hyde's five major methods of sabotaging self-discipline, you can see also that each one is a fraudulent, self-defeating form of *self-talk*.

Remember: Hyde constantly uses negative self-talk to sabotage you.

In other words, you'll find yourself transmitting negative messages to yourself when you most need to be self-supportive of your efforts. If you succumb to the part of you that secretly doesn't want this program to work, then Hyde will provide hundreds of counter-productive reasons and actions. But if you *listen to the part of you that desires self-discipline*, then you'll soon discover the rewards, joys, and accomplishments that self-discipline has in store for you.

Important . . . Important . . . Important . . .

Do not think of Hyde as an enemy. Such thinking puts you into a combative state of mind, into an inner conflict with yourself. When you fight against yourself, you lose valuable energy that could be used in the drive toward accomplishing your goals. Think of Hyde as an unruly child living inside you. This little kid has no self-discipline, no self-restraint, and no ability to delay gratification. Like any little kid, Hyde will be manipulative to get what Hyde wants. Don't try to crush this side of yourself, it won't work. You'll simply end up being a walking mass of inner conflicts. Moreover, the Hyde side of your personality is also the source of your playfulness and creativity. So, *think of Hyde as a part of you that can be won over by cooperation and compromise, not combat.* You'll learn more about how to do that later.

But for now you will do well to recognize that positive, self-supporting self-talk is your most effective first step toward counteracting Hyde's Frauds.

Remember: You can override Hyde's manipulative negative messages by replacing them with positive messages.

So, when you find yourself being cynical, escapist, etc., call yourself on it. *Consciously talk to yourself about it.* The more you do it, the better you'll become at it. Any regularly practiced thought, feeling, or behavior soon becomes habit. At this point you might be saying, "Sure, I've heard of self-talk before, but how exactly do I do it?" You are about to learn one of the most powerful tools in your self-discipline system. You'll use it for the rest of your life!

3.
Action-oriented
Self-talk

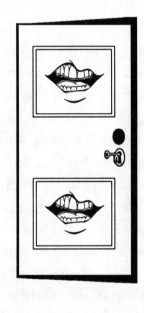

Action-oriented Self-talk

Now that you have an understanding of how the Hyde side of your psychological makeup works, you need to thoroughly familiarize yourself with the powerful simplicity of action-oriented self-talk.

Although just about everyone has heard of self-talk, few people actually know how it works. When it comes to self-talk, limited knowledge is almost as useless as no knowledge. Self-talk is a powerful tool that can be used successfully to deal with Hyde's tactics. To make self-talk work for you, you need to know its three basic requirements. It must be *Positive, Specific,* and *Present Tense*.

With that said, let's take a look at the overall self-talk process. Self-talk always goes on, even when you don't consciously hear it. That's right, you constantly receive messages from yourself, they never stop. Every second of your day you make choices based on these messages. Whether you are deciding what to eat, what to wear, or what to do, a process of choice is taking place. The choices that determine your actions are based on self-talk.

Self-talk is a conversation you have with yourself. Often, this occurs subconsciously. This inner conversation is comparable to the background music that plays while you shop in a super-market. The music plays but you don't really hear it unless you consciously and purposely focus your attention on it. But even though you aren't *consciously* aware of it, this background music has an effect on your behavior. Why does your local super-market play background music while the customers roam the aisles? Research has shown time and time again that background music influences our buying patterns. The stores wouldn't do it if it didn't increase sales.

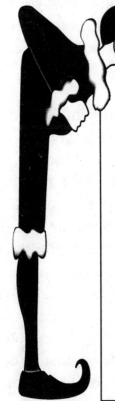

Did you hear about the fellow who returned a shirt to the clothing store and told the salesman, "After I got home, I realized that I don't like this shirt. I just liked the song that was playing in the store when I bought it."

Subconsciously, there are debates going on within us that we seldom actually hear, but that severely influence our thoughts, feelings, and behavior. Sometimes Hyde wins a subconscious debate that we didn't even know was taking place. This is precisely why you often find yourself doing things that you don't really want to do, or conversely, not doing things that you do want to do. Have you ever said to yourself, "I don't know why I did that." Get the idea?

In other words, your behavior is constantly being influenced without your being aware of it. When you find yourself having difficulty with self-discipline, it's because Hyde is conducting *secret* debates. Have you ever started to watch television rather than work on an over-due task that you had been putting off? This happens because the part of you that wants to get the task done didn't get a chance to join in on the debate. Hyde, you see, has played the game of backroom politics on you. That's how Hyde works, subconsciously, in the backroom of your mind.

When you consciously say to yourself, "Heck, I've just got to get that closet organized," the subconscious debate begins. Hyde, the part of you that doesn't want self-discipline, goes into action subconsciously. The votes are secretly cast, and two hours later you find yourself sitting on the sofa watching the conclusion of a bad television movie, and wondering why you didn't spend those two hours putting the closet in order, or working on a report, or putting together your diet plan.

The conscious part of you that wanted to be productive didn't get an opportunity to influence your behavior.

Remember: Hyde works subconsciously.

So, how can you expect to win a debate when you don't hear half of it? You can't! In order to counteract Hyde's influence, you need to turn up the volume on your subconscious self-talk. You can then begin to program your subconscious mind to support, rather than inhibit, your efforts at accomplishing your goals. That's the only way to diminish Hyde's control.

By replacing self-defeating subconscious messages with positive, specific, present tense messages, you will find that your powers of self-discipline are instantly improved. Believe me, *this simple concept will change your life*. I've seen people who tried this for a week surprise themselves with their accomplishments. Later you'll learn about other self-discipline tools to combine with action-oriented self-talk.

The main reason you're learning about self-talk first is because you'll need to use it immediately in your dealings with Hyde during the early stages of this self-discipline development program. Self-talk will be even more powerful when you begin to combine it with the other tools you'll learn about later. But for now let's look at the specifics of how action-oriented self-talk works.

Self-talk:
What do you say and how do you say it?

Action-oriented self-talk overrules self-defeating self-talk by being *Positive, Specific,* and *Present Tense*.

Why? Your subconscious mind believes whatever you tell it. It looks to you for reality. If you tell it that, "I am now working on my report," then your subconscious mind will turn all its attention to your report, no matter what you actually are doing when you say it.

The subconscious mind understands only the concept of *present tense*. So whatever message it receives that is stated in the present tense, it believes. Then it directs all your inner resources toward carrying out that message.

If your conscious self-talk says, "I *should* work on my report," or "I *ought* to work on my report," then the message your subconscious hears is, "I am *not* currently working on my report." So it doesn't move you toward working on your report. Moreover, while you are saying to yourself, "I *should* work on my report," Hyde is sending a present tense message that says, "I am *now* watching television."

You need to know that your subconscious mind sends messages to your motor functions, emotions, and other members of your physical and psychological network.

If your subconscious mind believes that you are currently working on a report, then that's what your feet, hands, and every other part of your body want to be doing. Simultaneously, your subconscious mind will focus on ways to put your report together.

Let's say that you are engaged in an activity you consider a misuse of your time. Let's say, for instance, that you are reading a magazine. Then you begin to think that writing a letter would be a better use of your time. Hyde then says subconsciously, "I am reading a magazine." Every time you consciously think of writing the letter, Hyde subconsciously repeats, "I am reading a magazine."

Your subconscious mind believes what you tell it. So, if you begin to repeat "I am writing a letter," then your subconscious mind will focus your attention, physical and mental, on writing the letter. As your hands hold the magazine, they will begin to feel agitated. Your feet will want to move you toward whatever supplies you need to write the letter. Your mind will begin composing the letter. Your whole being will go into a state of agitation and conflict, and won't settle down *until you are actually writing the letter.* As long as you repeat your positive, specific, present-tense self-talk message, you will feel compelled to write the letter; no other activity can satisfy you.

But beware!

Hyde, realizing that the "I am reading a magazine," message is not getting through, will begin to employ one or more of the diversionary poisons (cynicism, negativism, etc.) that we discussed earlier. Guess what? To be effective, Hyde's ploy needs to implement self-talk. But because you now are aware of what Hyde is saying, you can dispute that message and repeat *your* message over and over, and overrule Hyde's message. Your subconscious mind will respond to only one message at a time. Try it. As you repeat your message over and over to your subconscious, observe how your body and mind respond. You'll be surprised.

Important:

Repetition is the key to success. The more you repeat your message, the harder your subconscious mind will work toward your desires. Hyde is good at self-talk. But with practice, you soon will be even better.

Remember, in using the self-talk technique, you need to state to your subconscious mind exactly what you want to be doing, *as if you are actually already doing it.* Your subconscious mind works toward making outer reality match inner reality. So, upon receiving your message, your subconscious mind will direct all of your resources toward *making whatever you tell it become a reality.* You will be amazed at what happens when you repeatedly, forcefully, and positively state to your subconscious mind what you want to do, be, or have as if it were already a reality. This works with both short term and long term goals. And remember, in order to be effective, action-oriented self-talk must be *Positive, Specific,* and *Present Tense.*

Hey! Watch your language!

The way you use words during self-talk has a tremendous impact on whether your subconscious mind works for you or against you. For instance when you say, "I can't...," rather than, "I choose not to...," you convey to your subconscious mind that you have no choice in the situation. This creates a helpless attitude about your behavior and weakens your resolve. "I choose..." implies that you have a choice in the matter. Likewise, when you say "I *must*...," and "I *have to*...." you are telling your subconscious mind that you have no control over your behavior, that someone or something outside yourself is in the driver's seat. This does not *enthusiastically* work to move you toward your goals. Therefore, always say "I *choose* to...," which, after all, usually is the truth of the matter.

Also, beware of using "I *should*...." It implies to your subconscious mind that your choice of behavior is being made from a position of guilt, which serves to undermine your self-discipline power.

Remember: It's "I *choose* ..." When your subconscious mind hears your priorities stated in a forceful, positive manner, it feels your power. It then uses that power to mobilize your inner resources toward achieving your priorities. In other words, words count.

*A **final tip:*** If you state your self-talk messages *aloud*, then they will be even stronger because your message will involve two physical components, speech and hearing. Your messages will have the power and support of not only your mental network, but also your physical network. All the muscles and motor functions that are involved in your speaking and hearing will be activated and enlisted in the process of moving you toward doing your desired activity. In other words, the more parts of yourself you involve in your self-talk, the more powerful the message will be to your subconscious mind. And, in turn, your subconscious mind will have more strength to support the actions you desire.

4.
Understanding
Self-Discipline

What Is Self-Discipline?

I usually kick off my self-discipline seminars, workshops, and classes by having participants explore their feelings and ideas about self-discipline. Frequently, one's beliefs about self-discipline will dictate one's behavior.

Do you think self-discipline difficulty is caused by:

> ▶ lack of time management skills
> ▶ lack of organizational skills
> ▶ lack of ambition
> ▶ lack of concrete goals
> ▶ lack of motivation
> ▶ indecisiveness
> ▶ tendency to procrastinate
> ▶ laziness

All of these ideas surface when people are asked about self-discipline problems. With which ones do you agree? No matter, because they all represent *symptoms* of self-discipline difficulties rather than *causes*. In this program you will deal with causes.

At this very moment, even as you read, you are getting at the root of the problem, rather than pursuing changes that provide only temporary relief from symptoms. The common surface symptoms disappear automatically as you confront the deeper causes of self-discipline difficulties.

Indeed, you are making changes that will last a lifetime. To continue making those positive changes you'll need to understand the true nature of self-discipline.

Before you can develop self-discipline, you must first understand what it is. Ironically, the first step toward understanding what it is, lies in knowing what it isn't.

Self-discipline is not:

☞ A personality trait that either you have or you don't have.

☞ Forcing yourself to overcome your own resistance to action by using will power.

Self-discipline is:

☞ A skill that can be learned.

☞ Becoming aware of your subconscious resistances to action, then overcoming those resistances.

☞ The process of coordinating your conscious and subconscious psychological elements.

Your personality is a network of individual but connected elements—desires, emotions, needs, fears, thoughts, intellect, memories, imagination and others. In all human beings these elements operate in various degrees of conflict. Sometimes our emotions pull us in one direction while our intellect pulls us in another. Sometimes our desires try to lead us down a certain path but our fears won't allow us to follow.

Self-discipline, then, is the skill to direct and regulate all the various parts of our personality so that rather than being immobilized by inner conflict, all of our psychological elements are pulling together in the same direction—toward your consciously chosen goals.

Self-discipline is the process of psychological self-management, rather than a single personality trait. Think of self-discipline as the director of a play who gives instructions to individual actors. Think of self-discipline as the conductor of a symphony who insures that the individual musicians all are playing in harmony.

When you're experiencing difficulty with self-discipline, the question to ask yourself isn't "How can I get myself to do what I should do?" Instead, ask yourself "How can I get myself to do what a part of me doesn't want to do?"

The Key to Self-Discipline:

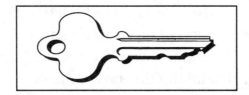

Regardless of whether you're trying to stay on a diet, clean out the garage, or be more productive in your occupation, the secret to success revolves around your ability to recognize and deal with the part of you that offers resistance.

While you're growing up you're told what to do by parents, teachers, and other authority figures. If you go on to college you're governed by professors. When you get a job, you have a boss. The discipline provided by these types of authority figures does not depend on whether we are in total agreement with what is asked of us. Usually, we are told what to do, how to do it, and when to have it done.

Under these circumstances, we don't have to struggle with any inner resistance. Therefore our self-discipline muscle doesn't get exercised. Without exercise self-discipline becomes weak and flabby. Then, in situations where we are called upon to be our own boss, we seem powerless to overcome contrary inner influences, both conscious and subconscious. Therefore, the part of us that doesn't want to be disciplined takes control of our behavior.

In other words, you don't tell your boss at work, "No, I don't think I'll do what you want me to do. I think I'll watch TV instead." But if you're your own boss, you'll repeatedly come up with such resistance to your own directives to yourself. You'll let yourself off the hook and say, "I'll do it tomorrow."

Because we've spent much of our lives being disciplined by others, we seldom develop the necessary skills to discipline ourselves. Again, self-discipline is like a muscle; it needs be developed and exercised in order to be strong, to be available when we need it. Unfortunately, as we age, certain psychological roadblocks occur that inhibit the development of self-discipline.

You can't develop the psychological qualities required for self-discipline until you've become aware of, and busted through these mental blocks.

Block Busting

Self-discipline requires facing certain realities about ourselves that we'd just as soon ignore. For instance, you might be surprised to learn that various types of fears are our greatest roadblocks to self-discipline.

Fears create attitudes that produce such ailments as procrastination, poor time management skills, and task avoidance. There are, of course, all types of fears. And, yes, we all harbor some personal fears that affect our behavior in varying ways and degrees. But certain, specific, subconscious fears create roadblocks between us and self-discipline. This is an unavoidable reality that needs to be accepted by anyone trying to bust through the roadblocks.

Subconscious fears are deep-rooted inner reservations that we often hide from ourselves. They play a spoiler role in all areas our lives. Moreover, in order to root out these buried fears, we must dig like hyperactive gophers. Why? Because:

▶ Facing our fears, either conscious or subconscious fears, creates anxiety. Anxiety is a powerful, uneasy feeling that we all try to avoid at any cost, including self-deception.

▶ We've been conditioned to view fear as a form of weakness or inadequacy. We'd rather rationalize than say "I'm afraid."

▶ We associate fear with childishness. "Don't be afraid, be a big boy." "Chicken?" "I dare ya." "Whatsa matter, Scaredicat, afraid?"

▶ Most of us believe in our heart of hearts that if we avoid an unpleasant or difficult situation long enough it eventually will go away.

Until you become aware of certain subconscious fears, and accept them as a part of being human, you'll never be able to establish consistent self-discipline. Subconscious fears will prevent you from transforming your ideas into actions. You can't possibly do anything to relieve yourself of these fears if you don't bring them into the light.

So, let's forge ahead, learn the various faces of these pesky fears, and reduce their influences on our behavior. Notice that I didn't say "rid ourselves of them." I said, "reduce their influences on our behavior." Again, fears are a part of being human. So, we need to accept them as a part of life. Only by recognizing and accepting them can we begin to minimize their immobilizing influence. While we won't ever be completely free of all fears, we don't have to be controlled by them. To paraphrase a famous quote: The worst thing we have to fear is fear itself.

Following are the most troublesome and common fears that block us from self-discipline. We all suffer them in various degrees. Get to know how each one operates. The more you know about them the better your chances are of minimizing their influence.

▶ *Fear of Failure*

▶ *Fear of Success*

▶ *Fear of Rejection*

▶ *Fear of Mediocrity*

▶ *Fear of Risks*

In the next part of this book, you will begin your ten day program. You will spend a few minutes a day learning to understand these critical roadblocks to self-discipline.

Over the next five days, you will learn about specific subconscious fears and about how each one acts to block self-discipline. Then you will do an exercise designed to give you a personal insight into how these blocks affect you.

Part Two

The Ten Day
Self-Discipline
Development System

Before You Begin!

The information in this section is accompanied by exercises that involve writing. Although each exercise is different, some general instructions apply to all of them:

- ☞ Be brief, no more than 15 minutes per exercise.
- ☞ Be specific, name names.
- ☞ Be honest, only you will see your responses. After completing each exercise, read over your responses and ask yourself how you feel as you read them. Then, if you are even remotely concerned about privacy, immediately destroy what you wrote.

Important: Don't just think about the exercises; actually write your responses. Don't let Hyde talk you out of doing the exercises. It is enormously important that in addition to your intellect, you involve your physical motor system in this part of your self-discipline program. The physical act of writing activates and involves your physical motor system, thus incorporating more of your whole self into the self-discipline process.

Moreover, the point of the exercises is to get you to explore your feelings about certain attitudes that commonly subvert self-discipline. Your doing the exercises will provide you with invaluable insights about when, where, and from whom you might have picked up these feelings and attitudes.

Knowing the past sources of your current thoughts and feelings is important because thoughts and feelings lead to behavior, and behavior, in turn, leads to thoughts and feelings. All aspects of your self are connected. These exercises were designed to simultaneously incorporate your feelings, thoughts, and behavior into your self-discipline development program. The more parts of yourself you involve, the more committed you'll be.

Let's get going! ☞

5.
Day One
Fear of Failure

Fear of Failure

Most of us have experienced fear of failure. It's a common psychological phenomenon. In fact, study after study has shown that the greatest obstacle to personal success is fear of failure. Do you find it surprising that even though we all want success, our first concern is not to fail? Indeed, we all harbor fears regarding failure. What most of us don't realize, however, is that these fears are based on a self-defeating misconception.

Most people erroneously regard any failure as an accurate evaluation of their worth. That's why many of us don't pursue certain desires. The pain of past failures linger in the dark corners of our subconscious, never far away; always lurking, ready to remind us of the emotional pain and the worthless feelings that resulted from a perceived past failure.

Why do we view failure as terrible? We do so because psychologically we tend to connect the failed endeavor to our self-esteem. We don't separate the task from ourselves. "The task failed, so I'm a failure," we subconsciously tell ourselves.

We forget to tell ourselves that there's no such animal as a failure; no zoo in the world has a caged specimen. Sure, a person can fail at a particular task or project. But a person cannot be a failure. Moreover, a person can fail at the same task numerous times yet not be a failure as a person.

The fictitious horrors of failure that are etched into our brains subvert our ability to exercise self-discipline in many of life's arenas. And therein lies what we really fear about failure: Humiliation!

Consider: Writer Lillian Hellman, after having written a successful play, *The Children's Hour*, then wrote another play, *Days to Come*, that was severely rejected by audiences and critics. The play was immediately moth-balled. Taking the play's failure personally, Hellman was so emotionally devastated that she couldn't write another play for two years. Even after she eventually wrote one, she rewrote it nine times. Moreover, throughout a long and brilliant career, Hellman never got over the pain of that failed play. Many years later she wrote of the humiliation she felt as audience members walked out of the theater during the doomed play's opening night performance. In varying degrees, we all react to our failures as did Lillian Hellman. Rather than view them as evidence of experimentation and growth, we humans tend to experience failures as blows to our self-esteem.

 Now consider: During its experimental phase, Edison's lightbulb flopped hundreds of times. Did this make Edison a failure? Of course not. Edison saw each failure as taking him one step closer to success. Indeed, because of his attitude regarding failure, he was able to draw on the power of self-discipline in order to persevere. Edison's experience with the lightbulb graphically demonstrates the absurdity of linking failure to self-esteem. I suppose we could say that Edison saw the light.

Our egos have been trained by society, schools, and parents that to fail is something about which we should be ashamed. Consequently, in growing up we grew more reluctant to attempt anything at which we were unsure of succeeding; our subconscious thought became "If I fail, I'll look like a fool."

Because this thought process goes on subconsciously, we are not aware of its powerful influence on our behavior. But regardless of any task we attempt, when this belief is in operation our power of self-discipline lacks the full force and support of our entire personality. We're like a six cylinder engine operating on just four cylinders.

What are the personal results of such a scenario? Because of this type of thinking, it is easier for many persons to continue compulsive eating, drinking, or smoking rather than risk the self-imposed humiliation that accompanies an unsuccessful attempt to change.

Or consider the procrastinating businessman who can't get himself to promptly perform the tasks required in his work. In many such cases, fear of failure is operating. He fears losing face more than losing money; so he subconsciously tells himself that if he fails, it won't be quite so humiliating if he hasn't fully devoted himself. "After all," he subconsciously tells himself, "I wasn't really trying."

This same twisted, subconscious logic operates within students who can't get themselves to study or complete assignments on time. Ironically, while this attitude provides a pseudo-shield from the self-imposed humiliation involved in failure, it also plays a significant role in most failed enterprises. For unless one fully invests oneself, one's chosen task suffers.

Before self-discipline can be employed, fear of failure must first be accepted, then shown up for the subconscious saboteur that it is. When we drag fear of failure out into the light, we'll find that humiliation is at its foundation. We, therefore, must continually remind ourselves that failure is not humiliation unless we make it so in our own minds. Failure can be viewed as a stepping stone rather than a tombstone. Once this reality is fully accepted, fear of failure loses its power to sabotage our self-discipline.

> *The point:* Subconsciously, we all link failure to humiliation. Fear of humiliation hampers our ability to make a strong commitment to our chosen endeavors, the big stuff and the little stuff. Commitment is a necessary ingredient of self-discipline.

The following exercise will bring you into contact with your own subconscious feelings about failure and humiliation. These feelings affect you emotionally, intellectually, and even physically more than you probably are aware.

Now that you know the inhibiting power of fear of failure, you can see the necessity of minimizing that power. The formula for reducing fear of failure lies in your refusing to link failure to self-esteem. For when you perceive failure not as a tombstone, but as a stepping stone to success, you immediately multiply your power of commitment; this automatically strengthens your power of self-discipline.

Remember: Failure is a stepping stone, not a tombstone.

Exercise #1 - Exploring Fear of Failure

The following exercise is designed to help you discover your hidden concerns and emotions regarding fear of failure.

You will explore three past experiences that you perceived as failures, mistakes, or just dumb behavior. Recall these three experiences from any area of your life: work, love, leisure, etc. The only rule here requires that these situations or events must be the most embarrassing and most humiliating experiences that you can recall.

You will be tempted to take all of these three experiences from a recent time in your life because you still consciously feel their sting. But, do not. Instead, take two of them from your earliest memories. Explore your childhood. This will give you an awareness about how, when, and where your attitudes and beliefs about failure originated.

Like ghosts, past failures haunt us. Indeed, past experiences do affect our present behavior. By writing down your worst experiences, you'll be giving these ghosts concrete form. Then you can confront them squarely. This will be your first step toward freeing yourself from their influences.

Note: Be honest. Spend no more than fifteen minutes on this exercise. And, yes, it will be difficult to write down these experiences. Hyde will be peering over your shoulder and giving you a load of reasons to simply think about it rather than write it. So for you to feel hesitant and uncomfortable represents a common reaction. If, however, you forge ahead you'll be astounded by the results.

As you write take notice of yourself both physically and emotionally. *Physically:* Do you clench your teeth? Do any of your muscles tighten? Your stomach muscles? Neck muscles? Do you notice any changes in your breathing rhythm? Faster? Shallower? *Emotionally:* Do you re-experience the hurt? Do you feel frightened? Angry? Hostile? Embarrassed?

Again, it is important that you take note of your reactions as you complete each of the exercises throughout this self-discipline program. Your reactions will give you valuable insight into how much your current behavior is subconsciously affected by the past experiences you recalled.

Start writing NOW

Before you continue:

Did you actually write the exercise? If your answer to this is "NO," then you just had an encounter with Hyde and you were manipulated. Please don't continue until you have taken the few minutes necessary to complete the preceding exercise.

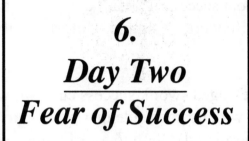

6.

Day Two

Fear of Success

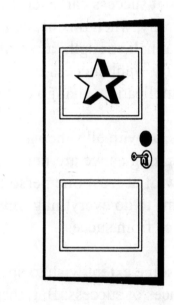

Fear of Success

Webster's New World Dictionary defines success as "a favorable result." Nothing frightening about that, right? So what's to fear about success? Doesn't everyone want "a favorable result"? Oh, if life were so simple. Unfortunately, however, it isn't.

Like a double-edged sword, success cuts two ways. We're all so enthralled with its good side that we tend to overlook its bad side. Subconsciously, though, our feelings regarding the negative side of success are very much alive. A subconscious negative perception about success can overpower our conscious desire to attain it. Naturally, when this happens, our powers of self-discipline operate at half strength; after all, a subconscious part of us does not really want success because of all the responsibilities and complications that go along with it.

With fear of success, as with all subconscious forces, we're powerless to fight it as long as we are not fully aware of its existence. We all know of at least one person who is his own worst enemy; who seems to do everything imaginable to keep himself at a safe distance from success.

Like him, we all to some extent wish to spare ourselves from the negative consequences of success. But, these negative factors from which we wish to spare ourselves are nothing more than shadows; when exposed to light they disappear.

Let's put a spotlight on a few anti-self-discipline shadows, the things we subconsciously tell ourselves that keep us from exercising the necessary self-discipline to achieve success.

Following are examples of negative self-talk that make it difficult to throw our full forces behind our pursuits.

"Maybe I don't really deserve success."

This type of attitude stems from feelings of low self-esteem, and is frequently related to feelings of guilt. We tell ourselves that we are not worthy of the happiness and satisfaction that come from personal accomplishments. We feel unworthy because of past or current behaviors, thoughts, or actions. This unworthy feeling usually is related to the unfulfilled expectations of others (family, friends, lover, etc.). Our transgressions can be either real or imagined.

Frequently such feelings grew from occurrences that we couldn't possibly have controlled. Then again, sometimes we feel guilty because we are guilty. But regardless of why a person feels guilty and unworthy, such feelings are responsible for much self-defeating behavior, subtle but effective self-sabotage.

"If I'm successful, people will judge me with a more critical eye."

Many people fear success because of the attention, both positive and negative, that would go along with it. They fear that they would feel a tremendous pressure to live up to their success. Many artists frequently go into panic immediately following a well-received novel, song, dance, or play. They say to themselves, "How can I possibly live up to it. Now, everyone is going to expect my next work to be just as great, even better." This feeling has thrown many artists into such a panic that they experience a creativity or productivity block, unable to work because of the success of their latest effort.

Anxiety about success affects everyone. We subconsciously tell ourselves that if we ever hit a homer we will always be expected to hit a homer. Then we tell ourselves that if we strike out after hitting a homer the boos will be louder, the disappointments greater, the humiliation deeper. So, rather than risk the strikeout, many of us find reasons (justifications, rationalizations, excuses) for not going to bat. Or if we go to bat, subconsciously we don't put everything into the swing for fear of hitting a homer and having to experience all the attention, pressure, and responsibilities that go along with being successful.

Most of us know that Babe Ruth held the home run record seemingly forever, but few of us know that he also held the strikeout record. And it is true that because of his success, people watched closer than usual when he went up to bat. But he knew that home runs could not be accomplished without risking strikeouts. Fear of critics didn't hinder his swing.

"It's lonely at the top."

How will others react to my accomplishments? " Will they be jealous or resentful?" We frighten ourselves into inaction by convincing ourselves that there are people who will react negatively to our achievements.

"If I am successful someone close to me will suffer."

A wife whose husband completed only high school doesn't follow through on her college degree program. A husband whose wife is noticeably overweight doesn't complete his diet plan. A man feels uncomfortable about a promotion over his fellow workers. A woman worries that having her own successful business will cause her friends to act differently toward her. A son experiences anxiety about out-earning his father. Each of these persons fear that their success will somehow hurt someone. This aspect of fear of success is particularly difficult because it is based on compassion for someone else, a trait that most us think of as positive.

"I'll be overcome by responsibility and pressure."

Subconsciously we tell ourselves that when the success starts, the fun stops. We tell ourselves that life will lose its joy if we began a daily exercise program, a diet, or any other organized routine. We tell ourselves that we will lose our spontaneity, that we will become boring and drab.

Get the idea? Each of the foregoing thoughts, actually self-talk statements, are based on imaginary catastrophes. They hardly represent the whole truth. Even so, they take a heavy toll. We all harbor secret, subconscious fears about the dark side of success.

We imagine untold pressures, overwhelming responsibilities, and many other frightening by-products of success. And so it follows: Subconsciously, we know that self-discipline leads to success. Therefore, we subconsciously fight against self-discipline so we won't have to face the hobgoblins to which success might deliver us.

Exercise #2 - Exploring Fear of Success

The following exercise is designed to help you discover your hidden concerns and emotions regarding fear of success. It will give you some insight about your personal feelings.

On a sheet of paper you are going to explore three past successful experiences that also created a problem for you. The only rule here requires that these situations or events must be what you considered successes at the time they occurred.

As you write about your three experiences, emphasize the problems that came with the successes. Take them from your earliest memories. Explore your childhood. Be specific. Name names. This will give you an awareness about how, when, and where your attitudes and beliefs about the negative side of success originated.

Note: Spend no more than fifteen minutes on this exercise. Hyde will be peering over your shoulder and giving you a load of reasons to simply think about it rather than write it. Don't listen to Hyde!

As you write take notice of yourself both physically and emotionally. *Physically:* Do you clench your teeth? Do any of your muscles tighten? Your stomach muscles? Neck muscles? Do you notice any changes in your breathing rhythm? Faster? Shallower? *Emotionally:* Do you re-experience the hurt? Do you feel frightened? Angry? Hostile? Embarrassed?

Again, it is important that you take note of your reactions as you complete each of the exercises throughout this self-discipline program. Your reactions will give you valuable insight into how much your current behavior is affected by the past experiences you recall.

Start writing NOW

7.
Day Three
Fear of Rejection

Fear of Rejection

A Story

Once upon a bright, sunny morning a man and his young son left their farm to make a trip into town. The boy rode atop their donkey as the father walked alongside. Along the road they encountered a fellow from the nearby village. "You should be ashamed of yourself!" the fellow said, admonishing the boy. "You ride comfortably while your poor, old father has to walk. You have no respect!" The boy and his father first sheepishly exchanged glances, then exchanged places.

As the two continued their journey, they chanced upon another fellow. "You selfish old man!" he said. "You take the easy ride while your poor son wears himself out trying to keep up. You should at least let the boy ride also." Not wishing to offend, the old man helped his son climb aboard. The pair then continued their journey.

Before long, they came upon a woman coming from the opposite direction. She, too, found fault with their arrangement. "I've never seen such cruelty! You two lazy louts are too heavy for that poor donkey. It would be more fitting for the two of you to be carrying the animal." Not wishing to fall from favor with the woman, the man directed his son to bind the donkey's front hooves together, then back hooves together. Meanwhile, the man himself cut a long, sturdy pole from a nearby tree. The pair laid the animal down, slid the pole through his bound hooves, then lifted the pole to their shoulders—the father on one end, the boy on the other, the donkey hanging upside- down on the pole between them.

Carrying the donkey, the pair trudged along. As they crossed the bridge that lead into town, the upside-down donkey saw his reflection in the water below from an angle that he had never before seen. The animal became frightened and suddenly thrashed about violently, causing the pair to lose their grips on the pole. Before they could grab him, the donkey fell off the narrow bridge into the water below. Still bound, the donkey was unable to swim. From the bridge, the father and son helplessly watched as their donkey sank out of sight, into the deep water below.

__Moral:__ After a moment of silent reflection, the father turned to the boy and spoke: "Son, we learned a valuable lesson today. We learned that when you try to satisfy everyone you end up losing your ass."

Because we all like to be liked, fear of rejection often becomes a dominant force in many of our lives. Unless monitored, our need for approval can put us on a long and endless fool's mission. Fear of losing favor with family, friends, employers, coworkers, or society is one of the most common blocks to establishing and pursuing personal goals.

Let's explore some of the ways this subconscious fear affects self-discipline. A couple of real-life examples will shed light on how fear of rejection works.

David, during childhood and adolescence, could seldom if ever please his father. As an adult, one of David's most vivid memories from his youth is one in which he was being chastised by his father for muffing an "easy play" during a Little League baseball game. David's little teammates witnessed the incident. He recalls the traumatic feelings of inadequacy, humiliation, and loneliness that haunted him for weeks after the incident.

Although less vivid and less intense, similar recollections of rejection color David's memories of childhood and adolescence. Consequently, as he grew into an adult his fears of displeasing his father grew into a general fear of displeasing anyone with whom he associated, especially authority figures, but often even strangers such as clerks, waiters, etc. Whenever he thought of putting his own desires first, before the desire's of others, a wave of anxiety washed over him.

Prolonged anxiety always generates feelings of inadequacy and inferiority, which in turn create a defeatist attitude. Such an attitude precludes the possibility of self-discipline. So whether David's chosen task was a diet or enhanced productivity at work, subconsciously the chosen task wasn't viewed as worthy because David didn't view himself as worthy.

Another example: Ann, as an adolescent, grew up in a tough neighborhood. She survived by being everybody's friend. Non-assertiveness, coupled with an extreme willingness to help anyone, anywhere, anytime earned her a feeling of security. "If they like me, they won't hurt me," was the message she sent to herself. Consequently, neither her time nor her desires were ever her own.

As an adult, whenever she attempted to follow through on desires that originated from within herself, inevitably she discovered that someone—friend, family, co-worker— usually caused her to abandon her plans in favor of something they felt was more important or appropriate. Because of her background, she had developed a reputation as someone who never says "No." Whenever she felt the urge to say "No" those old feelings of anxiety and fear surfaced, as if she were still the endangered school girl who had to please everyone to feel safe. Never saying "No" to others meant constantly saying "No" to herself. Self-discipline cannot grow in such soil.

Frequently, a person who subconsciously fears rejection doesn't consciously perceive it as a fear. Rather, this type of fear is perceived as a desire to be a "nice person." Persons in this position unwittingly spend an enormous amount of time and energy satisfying others and neglecting their own desires. They then become haunted by thoughts of "I never seem to accomplish what I want to," and experience feelings of unfulfillment. Unfortunately, this "nice person" seldom knows why she never seems to accomplish the things that she really wants to accomplish.

To develop self-discipline you'll need to overcome feelings of guilt, anxiety, and insecurity for saying "No" to others and "Yes" to yourself. You'll then find that your desires take on a greater importance, which in turn means that your inner resources will rally around your efforts at turning those desires into reality.

As you can see, one's inability to say "No" can have dire consequences. You will do well to know also that fear of rejection has a second face that reflects our subconscious terror of being told "No." Whether we risk hearing "No" to a job application, a marriage proposal, or a pay raise, fear of rejection rears its ugly head.

One of the chief reasons for a high frequency of drug abuse, emotional breakdowns, and alcohol dependency among artists, writers, and performers is that they constantly live with the fear of rejection. Indeed, to publicly perform or show one's art work is to risk having it rejected, maybe even ridiculed. Many artists feel, however erroneous, that a rejection of their work is a rejection of themselves. Because members of the Hollywood arts community have finally come to recognize the emotional toll of rejection, workshops and seminars that teach artists how to deal with it have begun to spring up all over Tinsel Town.

Perhaps because of their emotionally sensitive natures, artists are more susceptible to the emotional pain that occurs as a result of rejection. But, like artists, we all quake in the face of rejection, regardless of its form. No one is exempt. We all do our best to avoid rejection, even if it sometimes means engaging in self-defeating behaviors. Simply stated, being told " No" hurts. And because we are human beings, we don't like to risk being hurt. For some of us the prospect is terrifying.

We learn about the pain of rejection in childhood and adolescence; and it follows us throughout our adult lives. Fear of rejection subverts our ability to employ self-discipline because we feel as if someone is constantly looking over our shoulder, judging and evaluating us. Thus we find ourselves constantly second-guessing ourselves, our choices, and our methods. We then hesitate to throw the total weight of our inner resources behind our endeavors. This approach results in false starts and half-hearted efforts.

As a learned philosopher with whom you're acquainted said to his son as they watched their donkey drown: "When you try to satisfy everyone, you end up losing . . ."

Exercise #3 - Exploring Fear of Rejection

The following exercise is designed to help you discover your hidden concerns and emotions regarding fear of rejection.

On a sheet of paper you are going to explore three past experiences in which you did something you didn't really want to do, or you didn't do something that you really wanted to do. The only rule here requires that in these past situations or events, your behavior was based on a fear of being rejected by friend(s), family, coworker, or society.

Take your three experiences from your earliest memories. Explore your childhood. Be specific. Name names. This will give you an awareness about how, when, and where your attitudes and beliefs about rejection originated.

Note: Spend no more than fifteen minutes on this exercise. Hyde will be peering over your shoulder and giving you a load of reasons to simply think about it rather than write it. Don't listen to Hyde!

As you write take notice of yourself both physically and emotionally. *Physically:* Do you clench your teeth? Do any of your muscles tighten? Your stomach muscles? Neck muscles? Do you notice any changes in your breathing rhythm? Faster? Shallower? *Emotionally:* Do you re-experience the hurt? Do you feel frightened? Angry? Hostile? Embarrassed?

Again, it is important that you take note of your reactions as you complete each of the exercises throughout this self-discipline program. Your reactions will give you valuable insight into how much your current behavior is affected by the past experiences you are asked to recall.

Start writing NOW

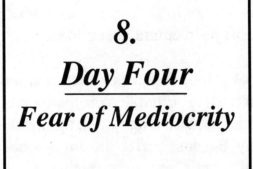

8.
Day Four
Fear of Mediocrity

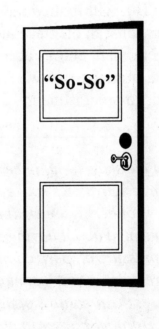

"So-So"

"So-So"

Fear of Mediocrity

How often have you considered yourself a perfectionist? Probably quite often. But how often have you looked beyond your perfectionism to try to get a glimpse of what is behind it? If you are like most people, probably never.

But if you took a long look at perfectionism do you know what you would find? You'd discover that perfectionism is the socially acceptable Siamese twin of a subconscious feeling called fear of mediocrity. Because perfectionism is socially touted as a positive personality trait, we consciously accept its existence within us as desirable. But within the hard-core perfectionist, fear of mediocrity stands unseen off stage and pulls the strings. So, even though perfectionism enjoys acceptance, it creates a pattern of self-imposed pressure that we tend to avoid. This avoidance, in turn, leads to procrastination and self-defeat.

An ice skater who once competed in a Winter Olympics spoke about the early days of her figure skating career. She lamented about having been so overwhelmed by the pressure of perfectionism that she had a nervous breakdown and lost most of her hair.

In another case, the pressures of perfectionism prompted writer Dorothy Parker to explain her inability to meet deadlines by saying that for every five words she wrote, she erased seven. Moreover, Parker's ongoing difficulties with alcohol were probably related to her intense perfectionism. These reactions to perfectionism are not at all uncommon.

Remember: Perfectionism is really a subconscious fear of appearing mediocre either to ourselves or to others. Attempts to escape our fears often lead us down self-destructive and self-defeating paths.

Fear produces anxiety, and anxiety produces a host of other undesirable physical and psychological conditions, including such reactions as alcoholism, drug abuse, and depression.

When we fear falling short of perfection, our self-discipline power suffers because we subconsciously send ourselves a message that says: "My efforts might turn out to be less than perfect, maybe even mediocre. Better not to even try than to risk that devastating possibility." In the meantime, while we subconsciously send ourselves that negative message, we're faced with the reality that perfection is impossible. Our self-discipline, then, suffers a defeat before we even begin our task.

Consequently, regardless of our chosen task, we fight ourselves every step of the way: "If I can't do it perfectly, then I really don't want to do it at all." This inner tug-of-war will shadow our every attempt to exercise self-discipline until we replace our subconscious fear of mediocrity with a realistic, rational point of view: Chasing perfection is like chasing the fountain of youth—it's a fool's mission. Immediately divorce your self-esteem from perfectionism.

Remember: None of us is perfect; nothing we do is perfect. We're all human; perfection is the domain of the Gods.

Exercise #4 - Exploring Fear of Mediocrity

The following exercise is designed to help you discover your hidden concerns and emotions regarding fear of mediocrity.

On a sheet of paper you are going to explore three past experiences in which you were held back by a fear of mediocrity. The only rule here requires that in these situations or events, your course of action was based on a fear of not doing something well enough.

Take your three experiences from your earliest memories. Explore your childhood, but you need to know that this particular fear grows stronger with age. So you might want also to explore your teen years. Be specific. Name names. This will give you an awareness about how, when, and where your attitudes and beliefs about being mediocre originated.

Note: Spend no more than fifteen minutes on this exercise. Hyde will be peering over your shoulder and giving you a load of reasons to simply think about it rather than write it. Don't listen to Hyde!

As you write take notice of yourself both physically and emotionally. *Physically:* Do you clench your teeth? Do any of your muscles tighten? Your stomach muscles? Neck muscles? Do you notice any changes in your breathing rhythm? Faster? Shallower? *Emotionally:* Do you re-experience the hurt? Do you feel frightened? Angry? Hostile? Embarrassed?

Again, it is important that you take note of your reactions as you complete each of the exercises throughout this self-discipline program. Your reactions will give you valuable insight into how much your current behavior is affected by the past experiences.

Start writing NOW

9.
Day Five
Fear of Risks

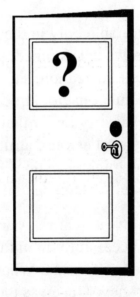

Fear of Risks

"Better to be safe than sorry," says a proverb that dug its way deep into our inner-most being during childhood. For many of us security and safety have become all. In areas where we have self-discipline difficulties, we've gone beyond simply following the old saying that advises us to "Look before you leap." In certain areas of endeavor, many of us unfortunately shy away from either looking or leaping. The unknown has come to be something we equate with danger. Like all the rest of our fears, fear of risks operates undercover. Our only clue to its subtle manipulation lies in its result on our lives: repetition that leads to stagnation.

Many of us feel comfortable only in the presence of sameness, things to which we've grown accustomed: same foods, same style clothes, same friends, same recreation, same, same, same. Life becomes a rut when we subconsciously come to view risks as dangerous threats to our security rather than as opportunities for growth. The only difference between a rut and a grave are the dimensions. But how, you might ask, does fear of risks interfere with the development of self-discipline?

I've found that persons who fear risks are persons who doubt their ability to function successfully in unfamiliar situations. The concept to focus on here is self-doubt. When self-doubt intrudes, your self-discipline effort never receives the very important "I can do it" message that supports its growth.

So while at first glance the connection between self-confidence and self-discipline might appear to be a loose one, it actually is a most important one. For as we learned previously, self-discipline isn't an entity unto itself; it is a collective composed of many diverse psychological forces which add up to a larger force, much the way that a tornado is a collective of little breezes that create an irrepressible wind by working together.

Moreover, our self-discipline muscle gains strength only through frequent exercise, exercise that leans heavily on self-confidence. So, if we live our lives in a rut, our sense of self-confidence falls into a state of atrophy, wasting away because of insufficient use. We seldom become aware of its loss until a situation arises in which we need it. We then discover that our self-confidence is useless to serve us. Think of self-confidence as you would a suit of clothes that you stored away years ago: You haul it out expecting to slip into it and cut the same dashing figure you did in bygone years, but you find that what hangs on the coat hanger is a moth-eaten, shapeless ghost of its former self.

Likewise, when you stop taking risks your self-confidence muscle won't be usable when you reach for it. Therefore you don't have the use of one of the most important elements of self-discipline: self-confidence. Furthermore, if a person continually refrains from taking risks, for even a short period of time, a subconscious fear of taking risks sets in. To address this fear is to awaken your sense of self-confidence, which in turn will give your self-discipline a psychological boost.

Remember: Self-confidence supports self-discipline.

Nothing ventured nothing gained. That's the ticket. Begin to think of risks as opportunities, not dangers. When you are faced with a risk that you wish to take, but feel immobilized by fear and anxiety, practice self-talk. Ask yourself "What is the worst thing that can happen?" Chances are, if you pursue this question, you'll find that your catastrophic expectations are probably exaggerated. Of course, this isn't an invitation to transform yourself into a foolhardy daredevil, but simply a method to get your self-confidence muscle into shape.

It needs repeating: Self-confidence and self-discipline feed off each other. No self-confidence, no self-discipline. You won't start that diet because you don't think you'll stick to it. You won't start that business because you don't think you can make a go of it. Indeed, a large part of self-discipline requires that you genuinely believe in yourself.

Remember: Self-discipline can be hindered by fear of risks, but this fear can be overcome by a change of attitude, which is entirely under your control.

Exercise #5 - Exploring Fear of Risks

The following exercise is designed to help you discover your hidden concerns and emotions regarding fear of risks.

On a sheet of paper we are going to explore three past experiences in which you took a risk and ended up sorry. The only rule here requires that in these situations or events you ended up saying, "I wish I hadn't done that."

Take your three experiences from your earliest memories. Explore your childhood. Be specific. Name names. This will give you an awareness about how, when, and where your attitudes and beliefs about taking risks originated.

Note: Spend no more than fifteen minutes on this exercise. Hyde will be peering over your shoulder and giving you a load of reasons to simply think about it rather than write it. Don't listen to Hyde!

As you write take notice of yourself both physically and emotionally. *Physically:* Do you clench your teeth? Do any of your muscles tighten? Your stomach muscles? Neck muscles? Do you notice any changes in your breathing rhythm? Faster? Shallower? *Emotionally:* Do you re-experience the hurt? Do you feel frightened? Angry? Hostile? Embarrassed?

Again, it is important that you take note of your reactions as you complete each of the exercises throughout this self-discipline program. Your reactions will give you valuable insight into how much your current behavior is affected by the past experiences.

Start writing NOW

Summary

Don't underestimate the value of the preceding information and exercises. Whether or not you're aware of it, positive psychological changes are already taking place within you. In the dark subconscious corners of your mind, you have thrown a searchlight on negative forces that have operated under the cover of darkness for years. Simply by becoming aware of these goblins, you have defused much of their power. In terms of your overall personality, when negative forces are weakened, positive forces are automatically strengthened.

Before moving on, make sure you're thoroughly familiar with all the subconscious fears we have explored. Don't forget that within all human beings these fears are present in varying degrees, and often operate simultaneously (yes, you can have a fear of failure and a fear of success). But even though you won't ever completely eliminate these fears, you certainly can minimize their influence. In other words, you can feel:

- ▶ *Fear of Failure*

- ▶ *Fear of Success*

- ▶ *Fear of Rejection*

- ▶ *Fear of Mediocrity*

- ▶ *Fear of Risks*

                                    . . . but forge ahead!

Tip: Write the above fears down on the left side of sheet of paper. Then write a number from 1 to 5 at the right of each fear. Number 1 goes next to the fear that you think you are most influenced by, and so on down the line. This is a simple way of imprinting your most influential fears solidly in your mind so that you can easily recognize them when they are affecting your behavior, thoughts, or decisions.

A SEMI-BREAK

You have been exploring the subconscious fears that put an unseen wall between you and self-discipline. You have recalled past experiences that play a key role in your present behavior. You now are in a better position to recognize these psychological saboteurs, and minimize the self-defeating influences of the past.

Now that you are building self-discipline, Hyde is about to pounce upon your progress with renewed determination.

 *Remember:*
A part of you does not want self-discipline.

To repeat: We all have a Hyde inside us. So, accept that in matters of self-discipline, we are our own most difficult problem.

Whenever you feel that Hyde's negative self-talk is slowing your progress toward improved self-discipline, go back and skim the section called "Meet Hyde." In fact, you might find it a good idea to do that periodically as a precautionary measure. It'll keep you on track.

Part Three

Subconscious Belief Systems

plus

Five Power Tools

Read this

Understanding
Subconscious Belief Systems

To further strengthen your positive psychological forces, and weaken your negative ones, you will now begin to develop an awareness of the underlying attitudes and beliefs that created the subconscious fears about which you have been learning. For behind each of these fears lies an irrational, self-defeating belief. Upon these beliefs, attitudes are formed. These attitudes, some of which we all subscribe to, determine our daily actions and inactions.

The following section of this self-discipline program provides you with information designed to make you aware of self-defeating beliefs and how they operate.

Important: You need to know that most elements in the self-defeating belief system operate subconsciously. So before you can neutralize their influences on your behavior, you must first become aware of their existence, then recognize when they are at work, then you can minimize their influence. In other words, to improve your self-discipline you need to shift your self-defeating beliefs from your subconscious into your conscious. Then and only then can you effectively deal with them. So, until you deal with your self-defeating beliefs, you will be plagued by never-started projects and half-finished projects; and you won't know why.

... plus five Self-discipline power tools

In addition to telling you about the subconscious beliefs that inhibit the development and application of self-discipline, this section will provide you with five power tools that will quickly build up your self-discipline muscle. But here is the key to using these tools: *Timing!*

To be effective, each tool needs to be used at a specific stage of the self-discipline process. Psychologically speaking, whatever you do (or don't do) happens in stages. When you consciously guide each stage to your desired outcome, you are practicing self-discipline. You may not be aware of it but during the self-discipline process you are applying specific behavior tools to get you started and move you along from beginning to completion. Self-discipline problems occur when people don't apply the appropriate tools that work best at a particular stage.

The main four stages of the self-discipline process are:

    ① *Decision to act*

    ② *Preparation*

    ③ *Action*

    ④ *Completion/Maintenance*

Most people wrongfully start the self-discipline process at the *Action Stage*, when in fact they are psychologically at the *Decision or Preparation Stage*. That is why so much exercise equipment ends up gathering dust in the garage, why so many diets are prematurely abandoned, and why so many business plans never hatch.

Why do so many people begin every new year with personal calendars, schedule books, activity organizers, etc., but stop using them in a few weeks? These wonderful tools don't work because people try to use them prematurely. These are tools for the *Action Stage*, but if the person using them happens to be at the *Preparation Stage,* these tools are almost useless. In other words, it is useless to use a screwdriver to sink a nail or use a hammer to turn a screw. Both tools can be tremendously helpful, but only if they are used at the right time.

Each of the five power tools you are about to receive were designed to be used at specific stages of any task you attempt, regardless of whether the task is a one-time endeavor or an ongoing life change. The success of each stage depends upon how much attention you paid to the previous stage. Don't attempt to built the penthouse before you build a solid ground floor. If you pay proper attention to the *Decision Stage* and the *Preparation Stage*, you maximize your chances of success at the *Action Stage* and the *Completion/Maintenance Stage.*

Remember: Self-discipline is a process with stages and steps, and problems occur when people don't recognize what stage they're in.

Important: The *Decision* and *Preparation Stages* must be worked on *before* the *Action Stage.* Later you'll learn about how the different stages work.

To repeat: Each day for the next five days, you will be presented with a brief explanation of a common subconscious belief that works against self-discipline. Also each day, you will find a description of a psychological power tool. Put these tools to work *immediately!*

10.
Day Six

"All or Nothing"
&
Visualization

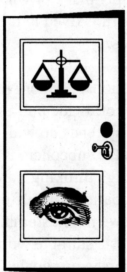

The "All or Nothing" Attitude

"There are only winners and losers."

"There is only one right way to do it."

"Either do it right or don't do it at all."

The preceding statements represent a belief that fosters self-defeating behavior. Every bit of research in human behavior reveals that life isn't simply black or white, win or lose, good or bad. Life, for the most part, is lived in the grey area, somewhere between the two extremes.

The prevalent but irrational "All or Nothing" attitude is what keeps gambling houses worldwide pulling in billions. The "All or Nothing" gambler always ends up with nothing. This extremist attitude spawns many of the subconcious fears we previously explored. "All or Nothing" thinking paralyzes our efforts at getting ourselves into a pattern of self-discipline because we feel, subconciously, that we might stumble. And because "All or Nothing" thinking equates a stumble with a fall, we feel that it's safer not to even try to pursue our goals.

Besides, under this belief system success means living a life of funless workaholism. Who wants that? Certainly not Hyde. And what about the part of self-discipline that says you need to break big jobs down into small, bite-sized tasks so you won't feel too overwhelmed to get started? Well, unfortunately, if all you can see is the whole overwhelming project, you will never get yourself to begin because you can't feel comfortable taking small steps; you must do it *All*. It's an "All or Nothing" proposition you tell yourself.

Since it is seldom possible to do any project all at once, you do nothing. Well, of course. With images of "All or Nothing" hanging over your head, you will find reasons to prevent attempting endeavors that require step-by-step self-discipline.

And finally, you subconsciously tell yourself that if your plan doesn't work, you will be *Nothing*, a loser. If you define yourself only as either a champ or a chump, then everything is defined in terms of life and death. This stress provoking proposition alone is enough to harpooon your self-discipline efforts. Under such terms, your inner sense of self-preservation will keep you from starting something that you might not finish. The irony, of course, is that you cannot possibly finish something unless you start it. And getting started is usually the most difficult step of any project.

To approach life in "All or Nothing" terms is to multiply your negative psychological forces tenfold. This means that in essence, you're working against yourself. This type of inner battle will drain you of the energy necessary for perseverance toward any goal. "All or Nothing" thinking is an important element in subconscious fears, which are self-discipline's greatest obstacle.

Power Tool: Visualization

Visualization is one of the easiest and most effective self-discipline tools at your disposal. It also works well as a time management technique. The best part about visualization is that you already do it. You do it when you remember something from the past, when you contemplate the present, and when you fantasize about the future. Visualization refers to all the movies in your mind. Subconsciously you use visualization thousands of times a day. Consciously you use it at least a hundred times a day. So, how does this relate to self-discipline?

All of your actions and non-actions are directed by the mental images that you create about your chosen goal or project. When you choose a goal or project, your mental images will either support your efforts or oppose your efforts.

> ***Important:*** Hyde's fears and doubts, the ones that weaken your self-discipline, frequently take the form of images rather than words. These negative images can be consciously transformed into positive images. Visualization is simply self-talk that uses mental pictures rather than words.

A few pages back you learned about verbal self-talk. You learned that the specific words you say to yourself are important in your self-discipline efforts. You know that you can use specific, concrete words and phrases to support every step of your goal or project. But words work with only a part of your psychological system, your intellect.

Hyde mixes the poisons that you learned about earlier with a variety of negative mental images and uses the mixture to side-track your self-discipline efforts. When this happens, you need to repeatedly visualize the positive aspects of your goal or project. You need to use visualization at every stage of the self-discipline process.

Visualization is self-talk in Hyde's favorite language. So to offset Hyde's negative influences. You need to *replace* Hyde's self-defeating mental images with supportive mental images. When you choose a project or goal, you can also choose mental images that make you less susceptible to Hyde's resistances while simultaneously programming your subconscious mind to motivate you and magnify your powers of perseverance.

Consciously create vivid mental movies that involve your senses. Let's say that your goal is to start rising an hour earlier to exercise. Then every day for a week or two *before* you rise earlier for the first time, visualize yourself doing it. *Hear* the alarm. *See* yourself stretching and rising. *Smell* the morning. Then *see* yourself doing specific exercises.

The key is to include many specific details in your visualizations. During the week prior to going into action on your project, *each day visualize yourself in action as often as you possibly can;* ten times, fifty times, a hundred times daily. Your visualization needs only a few seconds to be effective. Sure, it would be more effective if you close your eyes and visualize for thirty minutes each time.

But if you can only catch twenty or thirty seconds, here and there, fine. I repeat, practice visualization every day for a week *before* you go into the action stage of your project. Each time you *visualize* yourself actually doing your project, or the various parts of your project, you gain self-discipline support from your subconscious, and simultaneously weaken Hyde's ability to stall your action.

Visualization prior to action will firm up your commitment, increase your confidence, validate your ability, motivate you, and most important, it will reduce Hyde's influence.

In other words, the simple act of visualizing yourself confidently and adequately doing the in-between steps of your overall goal will maximize your inner strengths and minimize your subconscious fears and doubts. Visualization will enlist your subconscious mind to help you accomplish all the steps in your project. Once you get your subconscious mind working for you, it will continue working for you even when you are unaware of its supportive activity.

Remember: Visualization works best when you visualize all the specifics of the activity you want to do. In your mind: see, hear, smell, taste, and touch the location, clothes, room, temperature, details, details, details. Make it real. The more you practice visualization the easier it will become. So, mentally, many times a day, for a few seconds, use visualization to experience yourself doing what you want to do. Visualization is quick, easy, and remarkably effective.

11.
Day Seven

"I Must Be Perfect"
_&_
Reward Systems

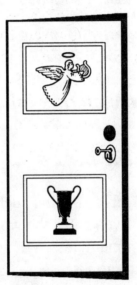

"I Must Be Perfect"

Earlier we explored a subconscious goblin called Fear of Mediocrity. Now we are about to examine the belief system underlying it: "I Must Be Perfect."

Perfectionism, as we established during our exploration of Fear of Mediocrity, reigns as one of life's greatest anxiety provokers. Its consequences include: procrastination, insecurity, alcoholism, drug abuse, broken relationships, and more. We all occasionally suffer bouts of perfectionism, when we find ourselves in terror of an error. But some persons find themselves in a continual wrestling match with this self-defeating belief.

"I must win this contest."

"I must perform this job perfectly."

"I must be the best."

Please notice that lingering behind such perfectionistic self-talk is the word *"must."* Even when the word *"must"* is unspoken, the implication is there nonetheless. Whenever you feel you *"must,"* you've climbed into a pressure cooker. You've fallen victim to the attitude that says "Any performance short of perfection is unacceptable." But human perfection does not exist.

A part of you realizes, of course, that the concept of perfection is only an ideal to motivate you to seek the best in yourself. Indeed, this part of you wants to develop ideas, plans, and goals then turn them into reality. However, another part of you, the part chained to perfectionism, refuses to let the ball get rolling.

Your logic tells you that no matter what you do, most likely it won't be perfect. For someone hung up on being perfect, the psychological pain, humiliation, and self-loathing that result from falling short of this impossible standard is too much to endure.

The consequences? Whenever the part of you that desires achievement begins to walk toward the door of self-discipline, the perfectionist part of you greases the doorknob. This behavior is an attempt by Hyde to avoid the impending anxiety that you have connected to imperfection.

The point: You will generate a lot more self-discipline and accomplishments by accepting that the "I must be perfect" attitude is a hindrance, not a help, regardless of your endeavor. "If you don't do it right, don't do it at all," usually means that it will not get done at all. But if you dispute this irrational belief whenever it arises, you will quickly come to realize that: The *reality* of getting it done is more satisfying than the *dream* of getting it perfect.

Caution: Hyde will try to keep you tied to perfectionism and away from self-discipline by telling you that, "You don't want to write a poor report, do you?" "You don't want to do sloppy work, do you?" You don't want to be called incompetent, do you?" Don't allow yourself to be tricked. Different projects, of course, require different amounts of attention, time, and effort. Trust yourself to know the necessary and appropriate level of effort you wish to put toward any given project.

Perfectionism weakens perseverance. And perseverance produces more achievements than talent, smarts, or luck. Indeed, the path to accomplishment lies in perseverance.

> "Nothing in the world can take the place of persistence. Talent will not: Nothing is more common than unrewarded talent. Education alone will not: The world is full of educated failures. Persistence alone is omnipotent."
> *Calvin Coolidge*

Here is a simple, enjoyable, productive exercise that you can use to teach your subconscious, which is where it really matters, that absolutely nothing bad happens if you don't do a particular project perfectly.

Try this: During the next few weeks purposely write a few mediocre letters to a few different friends. Do not try for wit, genius, or perfection; but do not say in any letter that you are just dashing it off. In other words, in the body of the letter don't make excuses for being less-than-perfect. You are not writing the Great American Novel. Do not tie your self-esteem to the act. Do not spend much time being methodical; the point is to write a quick, mediocre letter—and live. Any considerations about content are yours. Regarding length, keep it short. Again: By no means are you to acknowledge your purposeful mediocrity in the body of the letter itself.

As you do this exercise, you actually are reprogramming your attitude, both concious and subconcious, about perfectionism.

Power Tool: Reward Systems

Have you ever used a thoughtfully constructed, systematic reward system to help you get your projects started and finished? If not, then you will need to develop one. You are about to learn a simple system that will motivate you to action. This system will also reduce the conflict between you and Hyde when the time for action arrives, when you are actually faced with doing the steps that lead to your goal. But first, a word about rewards.

In the human behavior field rewards have been historically used to support desirable behaviors. Tons of research underscores the benefits of using rewards. A systematic reward is the golden key that opens the door to your self-discipline, painlessly. With that said, let's quickly address some of Hyde's mind tricks before they get started here. One of Hyde's favorite tricks is to start saying things like: "I don't deserve a reward for doing something that I should be doing anyway." "I don't feel right about giving myself a reward, it feels like a bribe." "A job well done should be reward enough for me."

Don't buy into it. Hyde uses such deceptive lines to prevent you from using the power of rewards to fuel your self-discipline. Do you feel bribed when you collect your paycheck from work? Of course not. And, unfortunately, "a job well done" will not reinforce your positive actions enough to insure that you repeat them. For that, you need the psychological motivation that only tangible rewards can provide. Successful self-discipline requires that you learn and systematically use the benefits of rewards. Believe me, rewards are the easiest, most effective psychological motivators available to get you started and keep you going until you complete your projects.

People who have attended my seminars, workshops, and classes greatly benefit by using a personalized reward system that includes: Private Praise, Contracts, and Gradual Steps.

❶ *Private Praise: Every time you perform even the smallest step toward a large goal, immediately follow you action with private praise.* That's right, immediately congratulate every positive thought, feeling, or action, *no matter how small and seemingly insignificant,* with supportive self-talk.

For example:

"It makes me feel good to get this done."

"Congratulations! You did it!"

"Good going!"

The beauty of this technique is that you can do it any time and any place. Over time, these little supportive phrases will begin to weaken your resistance to doing things that you *need* to do but don't really *want* to do. Give it a try. Soon you will begin to feel more and more comfortable when you take a step toward your goal. And by *immediately* patting yourself on the back following a completed step, you are boosting your self-esteem, which is a key ingredient in the self-discipline recipe.

Tip: Try to use the words of someone from your past who once gave you support for your accomplishments. Try to hear the sound of that person's voice. This will give you added subconscious power when dealing with Hyde, the side of you that does not want self-discipline. But remember, this technique is only one third of the reward system that you will be using. So do it a lot, but keep the words short and simple. Quick phrases like "Good work!" "Don't give up!" and "You can do it!" said in a strong, solid, supportive voice will work psychological wonders. This technique is too easy not to use constantly.

Important: If you slip in your self-discipline, *do not berate yourself*! Don't call yourself stupid, lazy, or stubborn. This type of self-talk is counter-productive, it's a subtle form of punishment and works to lower your self-esteem. Punishments do not change behaviors as well as rewards do. So when you slip, and you will slip because you are human, say to yourself, "So I slipped. No big deal. I'll do better next time." That's right, let yourself off the hook. And even though you might feel that you should be harshly criticized for slipping, the real truth is that you will be much better off in the long run if you do not punish yourself in any way. So, when you hear Hyde's put-downs, immediately replace them with a soothing, understanding word or two for yourself. And be sure to smile when you do it, so your subconscious mind will know that you really are not angry with yourself.

❷ ***Contracts:*** Self-contracts are powerful psychological devices that you can use to reward yourself for every step you make toward a goal. You contract with yourself just the same as you would with another person. When you contract with yourself always be specific about your actions and the reward involved. Sometimes translating the agreement into numbers helps.

For example:

"Every time I work for thirty minutes at a task on my to-do list, I will reward myself with thirty minutes of *guilt-free*, junk television, because I will truly deserve it."

"For every box I fill up and move out of the garage, I will put five dollars into a fund that will be used toward the *guilt-free* purchase of that new _ _ _ _ _ _ that I've been wanting."

"For every pound that I lose, I will put ten dollars into a fund toward that weekend trip to _ _ _ _ _ _ _ that I would love to take.

Tip: Simple written contracts with yourself will give you more self-discipline power than verbal ones. The act of writing involves you in your agreement physiologically as well as psychologically, thus adding even more power to your efforts.

❸ *Gradual Steps:* This might just be the most important element in any reward system. Remember that all of your self-discipline projects need to be based on a step-by-step approach, and each step needs to be rewarded. This holds true no matter how small the step or how small the reward. Because the first few steps of a project might seem too small to deserve a reward, many people make the mistake of withholding rewards until after they take the bigger, more visible, difficult steps of their project. This approach is counter-productive because it overlooks the psychological benefits of having a solid reward system that operates *throughout the entire project.*

In other words, use rewards at the beginning of the project, then when you hit the middle and end stages you will get a psychological boost from knowing that the *entire* project has had enjoyable benefits for you, not just the outcome. This can keep you going when you hit the parts of your project that are outside your comfort zone. It will also help you get started on your next project.

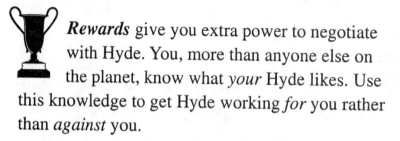

Rewards give you extra power to negotiate with Hyde. You, more than anyone else on the planet, know what *your* Hyde likes. Use this knowledge to get Hyde working *for* you rather than *against* you.

Exercise: Design a reward list

Now it's time to put together an easy reward system based on your personal pleasures. Don't just *think* about this exercise, *write* it. You will need it later. All you have to do is grab a sheet of paper and a writing tool. Then you need to list all the things you can think of that you would like to do for fun, I repeat, for fun. Think of movies, travel, classes, television, concerts, adult toys, clothes, small indulgences, big extravaganzas, etc. The longer the list the better.

When you initially run out of ideas the list is not done. You'll want to keep your list active. Add to it whenever you think of additional pleasures. Always add to your list as soon as you think of things. Make sure that each item on your list has a number on the left side. Don't concern yourself about the order that your reward items appear on the list. The important thing is that you keep each item short. One word, such as "Movie," works great.

Keep this exercise simple, don't make it a chore. You are talking about rewards here, so make doing the list fun! Generate lots of irresistible pleasures. Each reward on your list will be a powerful tool in your negotiations with Hyde. *So, do not take this tool lightly.* Your reward list is as important to self-discipline as any to-do list. Moreover, it is important for you to actually *write* your rewards down, rather than just think about them. We will be using your list in combination with the Action Plan that comes later. I repeat: A reward system is a key ingredient in your self-discipline recipe. So, use rewards generously and self-discipline will taste much better.

Example: Rewards List

My Guilt-Free Rewards

1. Go to a movie
2. Rent a video
3. Dinner at a special restaurant
4. Buy that pair of too expensive shoes
5. Fifteen minutes of long distance talk
6. Dumb T.V. with popcorn, one hour
7. Relax at the beach for one hour
8. Weekend vacation
9. Week vacation
10. Go feed the ducks
11. Entire video movie day
12. See a play
13. Fluff novel, one chapter
14. Fluff novel, entire book
15. Buy magazine
16. Read magazine
17. Play music, one hour
18. Go hear live music
19.
20.
21.
22.

12.
Day Eight
"I Can Achieve
Without Discomfort"
& Vitaminds

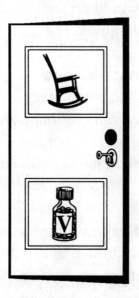

"I Can Achieve Without Discomfort"

"Maybe I will get lucky and . . . "

"Eat, drink, and be merry, for tommorrow . . . "

"Why put myself out . . ?"

These are the beliefs of persons who refuse to accept that there is no such thing as a free lunch. In order to achieve anything special, a person would do well to accept the reality that one must accept a certain amount of trade-offs.

Trade-offs can be viewed in terms of goods given for goods received. These "goods" that one gives can take many forms: time, money, immediate gratification, psychological comfort, or physical comfort—to name but a few. In other words, every journey to self-discipline requires that you cross the comfort zone border.

The person who refuses to venture outside the comfort zone, where trade-offs usually take place, can never hope to incorporate self-discipline into everyday life. However, the extreme concept of "No pain, no gain" does not apply here. Actually, the "No pain, no gain," attitude represents a version of the "All or Nothing" thinking that works against the development of self-discipline. Here, we are talking about the discomfort involved in such trade-off examples as: giving up sugary desserts when you're on a diet; saying "No" to various distractions when you have a project that you want to work on; or confronting an important but uncomfortable situation you would like to avoid.

And although all of these examples are uncomfortable, you would be engaging in "All or Nothing" thinking if you irrationally insist on telling yourself that they are *intolerable* rather than simply *uncomfortable*.

Subconciously insisting that everything be easy, without effort, is but another way to avoid confronting many of our secret fears and the anxiety that accompanies them. It is also a way to indulge the part of us that doesn't want self-discipline; the part of us that hates to wait or to work.

Whenever we find ourselves avoiding a particular task, our avoidance usually isn't based on the *real* effort involved in performing the task itself. Rather, our avoidance is usually based on a *pseudo-horror* that we have *subconsciously* connected to the performance of the task. Again, the subconscious belief that creates this type of avoidance is "I can achieve without discomfort."

The point: Learn to expect, accept, and tolerate periods of discomfort without mentally inflating them. Without periods of discomfort you will not accomplish even the simplest task. Moreover, practice identifying instances in which you act as if you believe "I can achieve without discomfort."

When you become aware of what you are *subconsciously* telling yourself, you can then *consciously* challenge your self-talk and replace it with statements that support your self-discipline. You will be surprised at how quickly your self-discipline is positively affected by using this easy technique.

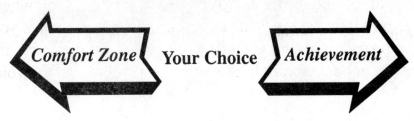

Comfort Zone ← Your Choice → Achievement

Power Tool: Vitaminds

The technique I'm about to describe will bring about fast and dramatic improvement in your self-discipline. I'm talking about affirmations. Affirmations are words or phrases that reinforce your goals or the steps that lead to your goals. They are like vitamins for the mind, or as I like to call them, Vitaminds. Self-talk affirmations work wonders, but *written* affirmations work even better. They provide you with simple and easy self-motivation that works on a very deep level.

Writing affirmations is a very dynamic technique because the written word has so much power over our minds. When we write self-messages down we are reading them as we write them, so it's like creating a double hit of positive psychological support for our actions, a vitamin for the mind, a Vitamind.

Now is the time to select a goal (or step toward your goal) to which you would like to apply self-discipline. Transform your goal or task into a short, single sentence, an affirmation. *Use your name, and write your affirmation three different ways using first, second, and third person.* In other words write:

▶ *"I, Ted Brown, practice piano one hour a day."*

▶ *"You, Ted Brown, practice piano one hour a day."*

▶ *"Ted Brown practices piano one hour a day."*

Keep your sentences in the present tense. Make them specific, sometimes using numbers helps with this. Try to capture an action when possible.

Always state your affirmations in positive sentences rather that negative sentences. Write, "I Francine Smith, enjoy life without cigarettes." Not, "I, Francine Smith, don't smoke." Write "I, Francine Smith, weigh 120 pounds." Not, "I, Francine Smith, want to lose 40 pounds." Positive sentences work better for self-discipline than negative ones.

After you have written your three affirmation sentences (first, second, and third person), copy the group of affirmations two more times, so that on your sheet of paper you have three identical groups of sentences. Each group should contain your affirmation three different ways.

Write your sentences *by hand*, slowly in a thoughtful manner. Don't just do it mechanically. Think about what these words mean as you write them. If you feel any negative thoughts as you write, or any resistances, or any doubts, then write down your negative thoughts on a separate sheet of paper. Even if the negative thought or feeling is only slight, write it down. Really listen to yourself. If, for instance, you begin to hear yourself say, "I'm never going to lose weight," "This is going to be too hard," or "I am never going to get the garage cleaned out and set up an office," write it down and then continue writing your three groups of affirmations.

After you finish writing your affirmations, look at any negative thoughts that you wrote. This process will give you a good look at the methods that you are using to inhibit your self-discipline. Try to connect the negative thoughts you wrote to one of the self-discipline road blocks we discussed earlier, such as Hyde's poisons, or one of the five subconscious fears, or one of the subconscious beliefs that underlie the fears.

Sometimes you will find that a negative thought or feeling can be connected to more than one of the roadblocks, sometimes connected to all three. After you discover Hyde's methods, give yourself a few moments to think about what you discovered. Then you automatically will begin to counteract Hyde's anti-self-discipline campaign. Your insights will help you develop positive patterns of self-discipline for any goal you want to turn into reality.

Now turn your *affirmations into Vitaminds*

This trick is quick and easy. Simply take the sheet of paper that contains your three sets of identical affirmations and separate the three sets. Put one set where you will see it every day, even many times a day. How about on the bathroom mirror? Your car dashboard? Your night stand? Next, do the same with the second set of affirmations. This will give you a set of affirmations in two different prominent places. Put the third set into you wallet or purse, so that you have it with you throughout the day. All you have to do is remember to read it as many times as you think of it. Ten times is good; a hundred times is better.

For the rest of your life, use this technique to turn each of your goals into Vitaminds. Try writing them on index cards. Change the cards every couple of weeks, or whenever you get so used to seeing them that they no longer have an impact. Change cards when you change goals, or when you add new goals to your life. In addition to making Vitaminds that keep your goals in the psychological spotlight, you can also make Vitaminds to help yourself start or finish any task that you don't want to do. This technique works even if you have two or three different goals going at once. Every time you write or read your Vitamind, you are giving your self-discipline a boost. Remember: Take your Vitaminds daily!

You will soon be combining your Vitaminds with Visualization, Self-talk, and other techniques. Individually, these techniques work well. In combination, they work incredibly well. Don't neglect them. They're all quick, easy, and effective.

TIP

Whenever you find an inspiring quote write it on a strip of paper and put it where you can see it many times a day. Also put a copy in your wallet or purse. Remember to read it frequently. Change your quote regularly.

13.
Day Nine
"I Can't Change"
&
Relaxation

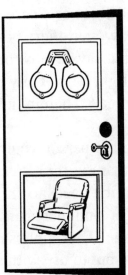

"I Can't Change"

"Some people just can't change."

"I'm just lazy."

"This is just the kind of person I am."

"I'm just like my mom (or dad)."

How often have you heard these types of statements? Probably quite often. But no matter how often you have heard them, they are as full of holes as a screen door. People do change—constantly. However, there is a catch. Maybe you remember the old joke that says, "How many psychotherapists does it take to change a light bulb? Only one—but the light bulb has to really want to change." Therein lies the rub.

No one can make another person want to change; the desire for change must come from within. In short, if a person is to change, then that person first needs to choose, *consciously and subconsciously*, to change. And increasing one's self-discipline easily qualifies as a change. This applies regardless of whether the self-discipline will be put to use with a small task or a big project.

About choosing to change: Our behavior, emotions, intellect, and just about everything else about us, other than biological considerations, are the result of a series of choices. Many of these choices are made on a daily basis. Moreover, we decide daily whether to continue honoring certain past choices; sometimes this process is conscious, other times subconscious. Indeed, choice is what links our current behavior to our past decisions, experiences, and influences.

We are chained to our past only so long as we choose to be. "I've been this way for so long, I can't change." "You can't teach an old dog new tricks." "I was raised to believe..." Such statements reflect an unwillingness to accept responsibility for one's present life. Of course, who we are and what we do today is related to yesterday.

But to allow our yesterdays to determine and dictate our todays and tomorrows is a choice. The part of you that does not want change wants you to believe that the past is a steel trap. If human beings were incapable of breaking free of the past we would still be living in cold, damp caves, and hunting for our food with a club. As a species we escaped being trapped in the past. We invented houses, automobiles, and supermarkets.

Likewise, we as individuals can reinvent ourselves by realizing that "I don't have to be who I was yesterday. Furthermore, I do not have to do what I did yesterday." By replacing negative self-talk with positive self-talk, and by using visualization to replace undesirable subconscious messages with desirable conscious messages, you will find yourself enjoying the many fruits of self-discipline.

Remember: While a positive attitude can create positive actions, the reverse is also true. Positive actions can create a positive attitude. They feed and support each other. You are now gaining the information, techniques, and tools to strengthen them simultaneously.

Also, this is a good time to alert you about the positive aspects of taking personal responsibility for your actions. Consider Shakespeare's observation that our faults lie not in the stars but in ourselves. Yet only a few of us ever accept responsibility for our predicaments.

We are not talking here about accepting responsibility for situations that are genuinely beyond our control; rather, we are talking about our refusing to accept responsibility for the situations that are well within our range of influence. And if we don't accept responsibility for our own influence on our lives, then we will subconsciously make all sorts of excuses that free us of the responsibility to take action toward our goals.

Moreover, if we rely on fate and luck to somehow deliver our goals to us, then we'd better pack a large lunch because we're in for a long wait. Good luck happens when preparation meets opportunity.

As Dick Motta, one of the winningest coaches in professional basketball's history used to say, "I'm a firm believer in luck. The harder I work the luckier I get."

Preparation
+
Opportunity   =

> ### *The point:*
>
> Your ability to develop, employ, and sustain self-discipline is directly related to your readiness to accept responsibility for creating your own circumstances.

Power Tool: Relaxation

By using some sort of relaxation system you can immediately increase your ability to think, feel, and do whatever you choose to think, feel, and do. Why? Any decrease in tension, anxiety, and fear, creates an immediate increase in self-discipline. And situational relaxation will immediately decrease the tension, anxiety, or fear that occurs when you are confronted with a task that a part of you does not want to do.

Now, in addition to learning a few basic ways that situational relaxation will boost your self-discipline, you will learn a quick relaxation technique that is tailor-made for use with self-discipline.

But first, let's quickly review how Hyde keeps you from applying self-discipline. By now you know that Hyde creates subconscious anxieties and fears whenever you decide to do something that takes you out of your comfort zone. When Hyde begins to use the poisons, roadblocks, and self-defeating beliefs that you learned about earlier, you begin to feel stress. Then the part of you that wants to apply self-discipline begins to turn away from whatever task is at hand. In other words, you begin the *Avoidance Process*: You begin to move away from the stress that Hyde connects to the task.

In this type of situation, avoiding the task at hand feels natural. Why? The *Avoidance Process* goes like this: First, you decide to begin a task that requires self-discipline. Next, Hyde uses various tricks to keep you from doing it. Then, because of the inner conflict that is beginning to go from simmer to boil, your stress level begins to rise. When your stress level rises, so does your anxiety level. Then, as your anxiety level rises, your motivation drops. Then you say to yourself, "I don't want to do this now." Then, because psychological stress causes a physiological reaction, suddenly you don't physically feel like doing the task.

In fact, the closer you move toward the task, the more you think and feel like avoiding it. As the Avoidance Process unfolds, you find yourself putting off, avoiding, or escaping a task that you need to do in order to reach whatever goal you've chosen. Then, when you start doing some sort of avoidance activity, you feel immediate emotional and physical relief. This false feeling of relief occurs even though you know that the consequences of your escapism and delayism will create problems later. What to do?

Well, you already know the poisons, roadblocks, and self-defeating beliefs that short-circuit your self-discipline. But *general* knowledge is not enough to overcome Hyde's resistance. You need to know which *specific* tricks are being used against you. Then you can usually pinpoint why they are being used. Armed with why, you can work out a quick deal with Hyde to relax the inner conflict that occurs when a part of you wants to do something that another part of you does not want to do. When the inner conflict relaxes, the roadblocks will begin to shrink, eventually becoming so small that you will be able to exercise your desired behavior. So how do you find out what Hyde is up to? Easy. All you have to do is relax.

Then you can ask yourself the "Why" questions: "Why do I want to eat something instead of writing this report?" "Why do I want to watch mindless television right now?" "Why do I think that filling out this form will be so painful?" "Why am I responding this way?" And although the specific questions that you ask yourself will change according to the task you are facing, the nature of the questions will remain the same. You will need to ask yourself "Why" questions.

These questions will help you quickly determine the real reasons for your avoidance behavior. These real reasons will inevitably be related to one or more of Hyde's various poisons or roadblocks.

Your recognition of these mind tricks will immediately diminish their power. *Relaxation is what gives you an opportunity to shift your behavior decisions from the subconscious into the conscious part of you mind.* In other words, when you become quiet and systematically relax, even for just a couple of minutes, you can suddenly hear yourself think. Then, by using your new tools and techniques, you can quickly transform your hidden negative thoughts into positive self-discipline support.

Important: *If you relax for a minute before beginning an avoidance behavior, then you will become aware of rationalizing, minimizing, and justifying the avoidance behavior.* This insight alone will give your self-discipline a gigantic boost. So how do you do situational relaxation?

A Quick and Easy Situational Relaxation Technique . . .

What is situational relaxation? As the name implies, it means that whenever you find yourself beginning to avoid a task that needs to be done, the situation calls for relaxation. Regardless of the nature of the task, whether you are about to write a report or start a cleaning project, a systematic relaxation effort will move you toward self-discipline. Physical relaxation will automatically create the psychological state that allows you to put your self-discipline tools and techniques to work. So, whenever you feel Hyde pulling you away from the task you want to do, take two or three minutes to go through the following steps. The more you do it, the faster and easier it becomes.

❶ Take a few deep breaths, slow your breathing, and say to yourself, "I am completely relaxed." It doesn't really matter whether you are standing, sitting, or lying down. Simply try to be as physically comfortable as the situation will allow.

❷ Then as you continue to slow your breathing say to yourself: "I am tightening my forehead, then relaxing it. I am tightening all my facial muscles, then relaxing them. I am tightening my jaw, then relaxing it. I am tightening my neck muscles, then relaxing them." Continue to go through your major muscle groups (shoulders, arms, hands, back, stomach, etc.) first tightening then relaxing them.

❸ Take a minute to really give your body a chance to feel relaxed. Control your breathing. Use your self-talk to support your physical relaxation. Use visualization to see yourself easily doing the task that is at hand.

❹ Quickly ask and answer a few "Why" questions. Listen to what Hyde is saying to you. Become aware of how Hyde is trying to trick you into avoiding the task. Then counteract Hyde's influence by telling yourself the other side of the story. Be convincing, be forceful, but be relaxed. Focus on a specific immediate reward for completing the task. Use visualization, self-talk, or any other tools that feel useful.

❺ Begin to take a small action step toward the task. As you get closer to the room, table, tools, or wherever you need to be to start the task, continue to control your breathing and physical state. Remind your muscles to relax. Every time you feel or hear an avoidance message from Hyde, use your self-discipline tools and techniques to replace that message with a flood of self-discipline messages. Pour it on thick.

❻ Actually start the first step of your task. Once again, remind yourself to relax. Control your breathing. And, I repeat, every time you feel or hear an avoidance message from Hyde, use your self-discipline tools and techniques to replace that message with a flood of self-discipline messages.

Getting started is the toughest part of the self-discipline process. While this is true with daily tasks like exercises, diets, and skill development, it is also true with one time projects. Situational relaxation, more than any other tool or technique, will help you start, no matter what type of project or task is at hand. Use this quick relaxation technique every day, throughout the day, and watch yourself sail through the self-discipline process over and over. Yes, situational relaxation becomes easier and easier with regular use. And, yes, you will complete more tasks when you systematically relax and stop fighting with yourself.

Note: Situational relaxation is especially effective in dealing with self-discipline challenges that involve consumptive behaviors such as smoking, drinking, and overeating. These behaviors become habits when we automatically react to a situation without first thinking about our actions; without really hearing ourselves give the order to act, without consciously knowing why we are choosing to act in a self-defeating way. Moreover, because consumptive behaviors seem to descend upon you spontaneously from out of nowhere, you naturally feel that this behavior is beyond your control. No so, not by a long shot. You actually are in control of your behavior, or more accurately, the Hyde side of you is in control.

Remember: Hyde is a part of you and is therefore subject to your influence. Relax and listen to what Hyde says, your behavior will then begin to make sense to you. And you can then come up with ways that will have you doing what you really want to do rather that what Hyde wants you to do. Remember also that consumptive behaviors need to be replaced with some other behavior or you will feel a void where the consumptive behavior used to be. This void will affect your self-discipline negatively. So whenever you attempt to stop a behavior, always replace it with another behavior that you would rather have.

14.
Day Ten

"Something Terrible Will Happen"
&
A Goal Sheet

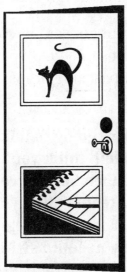

"Something Terrible Will Happen"

Open any psychology book and you will find at least one chapter that deals with the human animal's exaggerated fear of falling victim to a catastrophic event. This tendency is a psychological mechanism designed to keep us from harm.

Whenever we approach a situation in which we feel uneasy or uncomfortable, our anxiety rises from the depths in the form of an inner voice. This voice acts as a caution sign: "If you try this, here are all the bad things that could happen to you." So far so good.

But all too often the subconscious voice then picks out the worst possibility and begins to hound you with it. Simultaneously the voice reminds you of past similar instances in which negative outcomes occurred:

> **"What? You're going to talk to the boss about a raise? He'll think you're complaining and fire you. Remember, the coach of the high school baseball team called you a whining complainer in front of the team when you asked whether you could switch from right field to first base, and you never forgot the feeling."**

> **"What? You're going to give a speech? You'll probably forget the words, ruin it, and make a fool of yourself. Remember how you felt when you blew the pep squad routine in front of the student body assembly?"**

And so it goes, until you are immobilized by the threat of disaster.

Consider: This subconscious thought process occurs with all types of activities; riding on an airplane, going to a job interview, writing a paper or report, almost anything that involves risk.

Now consider: Every time you take a step toward a goal, you are taking a risk. Whether you are buying real estate, starting a diet, or cleaning out the garage, something can go wrong. So to spare you the possibility of catastrophe, your inner voice over-emphasizes the dangers involved in the risk. Unfortunately, however, listening to this over-cautious doomsayer will drain you of the enthusiasm and self-discipline needed to follow through on your desires.

Sure, in life real dangers do actually exist. But here, we are talking about the effects of self-created, exaggerated dangers that serve only to inhibit us rather than protect us. Remember, the belief we're looking at, Something Terrible Will Happen, operates in an extremely subtle manner. It disguises itself in many forms.

Do you have difficulty pursuing one of your goals because you began to feel anxious every time you take a step toward it? If so, look closely at what you are telling yourself about the goal that you have chosen. Only you will know when "Something Terrible Will Happen" is operating.

So, be honest with yourself about whether your procrastination is based on a catastrophic expectation or based on a legitimate concern. Don't let Hyde use you mental danger signals against you. Challenge your fears with your intellect. If you consciously listen to your *rational* inner voice, then your *emotional* voice will lose some of its power over you. Then, you can move along with fewer bumps in the road.

Power Tool: Goal Sheet

Everyone has goals. Unfortunately most people allow their goals to float around in their heads as dreams. Until you turn your dreams into concrete goals that you can actually work with, all they will ever be are dreams, unrealized dreams. You see, dreams never become reality until they first become concrete goals; then and only then will the goals have a shot at becoming reality. And there you have the difference between dreams and goals. So, first you have a dream, then you transform the dream into a concrete goal, then you devise a plan to reach the goal. This happens to be shorthand for the self-discipline process.

Now you are ready to add the Goal Sheet to your tool box. This tool is the quickest, easiest way for you to transform your dreams into achievable goals. No matter how large or small your goal, the Goal Sheet is a powerful tool that will put the self-discipline process into motion for you. The Goal Sheet plays an important psychological function. Its purpose is to give you direction, commitment, motivation, and a foundation for action. You will realize surprising self-discipline benefits. In fact, I recommend that you make a Goal Sheet for every goal that requires a concerted effort. For now, however, I suggest that you choose only one goal to work with.

Important: When you make your Goal Sheet, don't go getting all serious and tax your brain. Making a Goal Sheet should be a quick and easy deal for you. This tool is much too important to take seriously. So,

RELAX!

Exercise:

The Goal Sheet has 3 simple components:

❶   You need to write a *specific, detailed* statement of your goal. I repeat, your written goal needs to include *specifics*. Don't write, I want good health, or great wealth, or genuine happiness, etc. Instead write "I want to lose 30 pounds in 6 months," "I want to be earning $100,000 per year in two years," "I want to learn conversational Spanish in 1 year." *The clearer the picture of what you want, the easier it will be fore you to develop a plan that gets it for you.*

❷   You need to state why you want to reach this goal. What is your purpose? Some people refer to this as a sort of mission statement. Clarity of purpose determines the power of your commitment, which in turn fuels the self-discipline process. Writing down your purpose will also help you be sure that the goal you chose is really *your* dream and not someone else's idea of what you should do. Having a written purpose for your goal is an important part of the self-discipline process because it gives you enduring motivation. Indeed, for self-discipline to roll along smoothly rather than grind along in a series of frustrating starts and stops, *you need to know clearly why you are doing what you are doing.*

❸   You need to list the steps, as many as you can think of, that your goal requires. Later you will give each of these steps a time frame. But for now all you need to do is put down the steps in short sentence form, very short sentence form. Don't try to list the steps in order. Just write them down. You can always add, delete, or modify later. As you list the required steps, break down the intimidating ones into smaller steps. The smaller the steps, the better your chances of completing them.

Start writing NOW

After completing the preceding exercise, you will need to ask yourself some questions that will help you know, *really know*, whether this goal is something you really want to pursue and achieve. The questions that I want you to ask yourself will either solidify your commitment or prompt you to reconsider your direction. Either way, you will be better off knowing your true feelings about it. If the thought of pursuing your goal creates anxiety, don't be too concerned, Hyde might be whispering hollow fears to your subconscious.

Remember: Hyde doesn't want you to actually *do* anything that requires a trip outside of your comfort zone, which is of course where you will find lots of treasures. The following questions will clarify your true feelings about your goal. You need to know the answers in order to keep Hyde from playing successful tricks on you when you begin taking action steps toward your goal. Remember as you answer these questions that Hyde will be putting in an opinion. So be sure to look closely at any negative opinions that arise; is it you talking realistically, or Hyde playing games.

Now ask yourself: Is this goal worth my time and effort? Are the rewards worth the risks? How will my daily life be affected? Is this a good time? What is the downside of my pursuing and attaining this goal? How will my family, friends, and career be affected by my pursuit and attainment of this goal? You don't need to write down your answers, but you do need to give them some thought. *Your thoughts and feelings about your answers are an important part of the Goal Sheet tool.* Don't forget, keep it simple.

Part Four

Putting It All Together

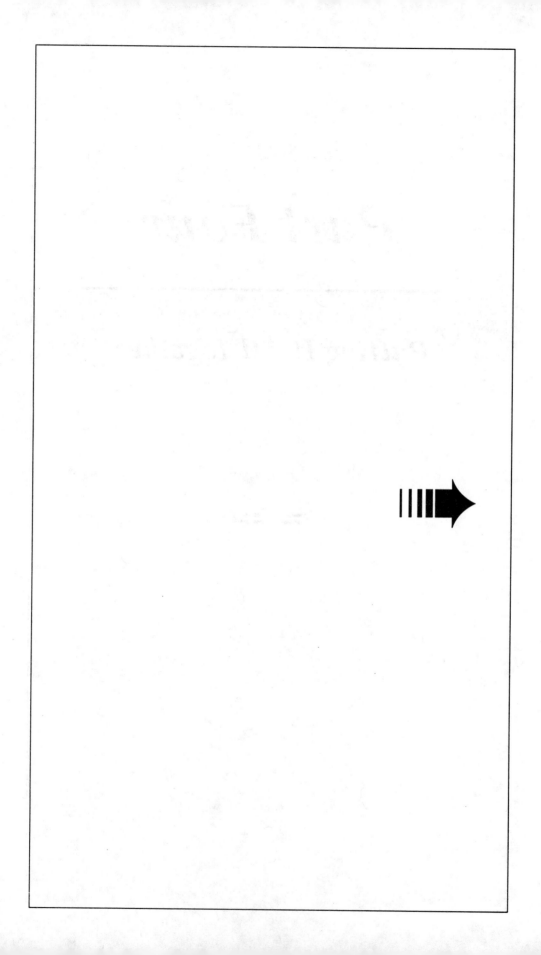

Congratulations!

Now you are ready to put your knowledge into action!

By now you know that self-discipline is a process, not an inborn personality trait. You know the psychological causes of self-discipline blocks. You know the self-defeating subconscious tricks that make self-discipline unnecessarily difficult. You also know about tools and techniques that will enhance your self-discipline power. And you know how to use them. But you don't know *when* to use them. *Knowing when is as important as knowing how.*

In fact, the key to successful self-discipline lies in using specific tools at the appropriate stage of the self-discipline process. So don't forget that the self-discipline process, regardless of the size of your task or the scope of your goal, occurs in specific stages. Again, certain tools work best within certain stages.

On the following pages you will learn about the stages, how they work, and when to use the various tools. In other words, you are about to receive a big payoff from all you've learned.

The self-discipline process occurs in 4 stages

❶ *Decision*

❷ *Preparation*

❸ *Action*

❹ *Completion/Maintenance*

Important: You need to satisfy the requirements of each stage before attempting the next stage. Otherwise, you are setting yourself up for unnecessary difficulties. By far, the most common mistake people make when attempting to use self-discipline is this: They select a goal and start at the Action Stage of the self-discipline process, before doing the necessary groundwork. That's like trying to build a penthouse before building the first floor.

I repeat, starting toward your goal at the Action Stage, before taking specific steps in the Decision Stage and the Preparation Stage, is putting the cart before the horse; sure, you might eventually drive your goods to market but not without driving yourself and your horse half crazy. You will make self-discipline a lot easier for yourself by doing things in a certain order. Believe me, this approach will save you a lot of time and trouble no matter what type of goals you choose, whether you are starting a business, losing weight, or finally getting the garage cleared out. Now, let's take a look at the first stage of the self-discipline process: Decision.

15.

The
Decision
Stage

Hummm . . .

Decision Stage

As the name implies, this first stage is where you choose a goal and solidify that choice. There is more to this process than you might think. On the other hand, there is nothing difficult or complicated about it. And while the steps in this stage are quite easy to do, they are an extremely important part of the self-discipline process. Failure to take the necessary steps here will usually result in self-discipline difficulty at the Action Stage.

During the Decision Stage your purpose is to build a psychological foundation, a commitment that will carry you through all the steps (hourly, daily, weekly, monthly) that your goal requires. A solid psychological foundation will empower you to deal with all the doubts, fears, and self-defeating beliefs that Hyde will send your way (hourly, daily, weekly, monthly). Ironically, the more important your goal is to you, the more Hyde will try to keep you from going after it. For Hyde, you see, an important goal appears frightening and difficult. Because of this, you will need to be aware of Hyde every step of the way. Self-discipline is easier when you know exactly what you are up against.

You need to realize that every coin has two sides. Yes, you can have a clean garage, but you will no longer have the stuff that currently fills it. Yes, you can have your own business, but you will no longer have the security of your job with the post office. Sure, if you stop drinking at the local tavern you will have better health and more money, but you might lose the company of your drinking buddies.

In other words, you will always have to give up something in order to get something. And while you consciously want certain things, you might subconsciously not want to accept the other side of the coin, the letting go of certain other things. I repeat: In order to get what you want, you have to give up something else.

Give up what? You need to answer that question before you go into action on your goal. A few examples of what you might need to give up: time, money, physical comfort, emotional comfort, security, leisure, a personal relationship, other goals (for now), self-image, parental approval, societal approval, etc., etc., etc.

Important: One of Hyde's favorite tricks is to have you believe that you must completely (All or Nothing) give up a certain something that you might not have to give up *completely* in order to attain your goal. Sometimes you will be able to find ways to keep what you have and still get what you want, sometimes not. Sometimes you can make compromises, sometimes not. These types of decisions need to be made consciously whenever you choose a goal, because each goal has a dark side that operates subconsciously. Hyde, the side of you that doesn't want self-discipline, will use your subconscious concerns like emotional rope to tie you to Delayism, Defeatism, Cynicism, well, you know the rest.

In the Decision Stage you need to bring all of your subconscious concerns to the surface in order to deal with them, so they won't ambush you at the Action Stage. Conversely, when you consciously explore both sides of your goal, "getting" vs. "giving up," and you are clear about it, then you can deal with Hyde from a solid position. If, however, you don't bring both sides of the picture into focus, you will be dragging an invisible anchor. You won't see what keeps you from moving forward.

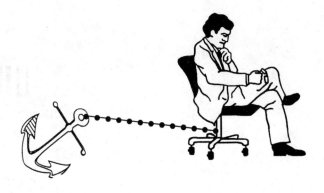

Exercise:

All you need to do here is write down your goal across the top of a sheet of paper. Then on the left side of the paper list the benefits of pursuing and achieving your goal. On the right side list the drawbacks. Nothing fancy. The point of this process is to make sure you bring all the negative aspects of your goal, and the pursuit of it, into clear focus. Also, take a look at your Goal Sheet, which has a list of the steps toward your goal. What must you give up to achieve each step? When you achieve

your goal, what will the down side be? Again, keep this process simple, but do it. List the benefits and steps on the left and the negative aspects of your goal pursuit on the right. Sound simple? Well, it is. Remember, this simple process will provide you with a surprising amount of self-discipline fuel. So always take a few minutes to do it with each goal you want to achieve.

After you do this process with your chosen goal. Then you will be ready to move to the Preparation Stage. I repeat, by completing the Decision Stage, you will move smoother, faster, and more confidently toward your goal.

Start writing NOW

16.

The

Preparation

Stage

Preparation Stage

Welcome to the all important Preparation Stage. As an Olympic Gold Medalist once said, when asked how she turned her average physical assets into a championship performance, "Everybody wants to win, but not everybody wants to *prepare* to win." She went on to say that dedicated *preparation* is what won the Gold. This concept applies to your relationship with self-discipline. Spectacular success comes from simple preparation.

Traveling from your desires to your goals, you will always need to go through a series of steps. So, when you decide to make the trip, preparation is a necessary piece of luggage. Preparing for action means that you need to make a *daily* plan. Your plan will, of course, contain steps that need to be accomplished by certain times and dates. Without question, self-discipline flows much better when you receive daily reminders about what to do and when to do it.

Moreover, self-discipline works better if the reminders are written onto paper rather than left floating in your head. All we are talking about here is a simple "to do" list. And, most important, if your written list breaks each task into small steps, you will find that your resistance to doing each task greatly diminishes.

Remember: Every daily plan needs to be a *simple* plan, an uncomplicated "to do" list. Unless you have a written plan, Hyde will overwhelm you by subconsciously convincing you that your goal is just too big for little ol' you to accomplish. But a simple daily "to do" list reminds you that every big accomplishment is nothing more than a lot of little accomplishments added together.

So, on your daily "to do" list be sure to break down each task into a series of small steps. This simple act will instantly transform intimidating tasks into friendly steps. Incidentally, this "simplifying" technique will help you get going again if you have been hit by a Hyde roadblock.

> *Self-discipline:*
> *It's a trial by the mile and hard by the yard,*
> *but a cinch by the inch.*

And, surprisingly, ten minutes of daily planning, making a simple "to do" list, will actually generate extra free time for you. I repeat: A simple "to do" list will give you access to hours of time you never knew you had. That new found time can be filled any way you want, work or play, your choice. So, if daily planning will give you more self-discipline and more time, then why not give it a try? It will be the best investment in self-discipline you will ever make.

But Hyde balks at the mere thought of your making a daily "to do" list, right? Well, if you promise Hyde that you will keep your daily lists short and simple, then you will see your resistances to doing it shrink. And by all means remember to use your self-discipline tools and techniques to keep Hyde from depriving you of this easy self-discipline booster.

A Daily "quick" Plan

A **6** Step Daily Plan

Here is a quick and easy method of daily planning that will give your self-discipline a real charge. Sure, there are many types of plans that you can use, lots of them are more comprehensive and complex than the one that follows. But the following plan is designed to be easy, quick, and simple. It is, in fact, designed for simplicity. And because it won't take much time and brain power, you will be more likely to actually do it: *Daily!*

❶ Look at your Goal Sheets and pick a goal. Do you want to work toward more than one goal? If the goals don't conflict, no problem. But don't overwhelm yourself by trying to do too much too soon. After you try this for a while and get used to doing it, you will find that pursuing several goals simultaneously isn't really that difficult. But for now you will do better to stick with only one or two goals.

❷ Choose a launch date when you want to begin action.

❸ Make a "to do" list for the day you plan to begin. Be sure to date your list. Write down a few of the easier actions you need to do in order to reach your goal. No matter what goal you choose, there is something you can do about it on the launch day. Then, next to each action step, whenever possible write a guesstimate for time it will take to complete each action. Don't just think about it. *Write it.*

❹ Next to each action step write, in abbreviated form, a reward from your reward sheet. This will help you recruit Hyde's cooperation. Don't just think about it. *Write it.* Remember that the most motivating rewards are the rewards that can occur soon after the completion of the action step. Make the size of the reward equivalent to the size of the step. Some people find it motivating to have a bonus reward when they do everything on the list. This will be your call. If you like, you can attach one large reward to several small steps. Again, this is your call. You will quickly find out what works best for you. Remember: Acknowledge Hyde, and Hyde will respond with cooperation rather than roadblocks. Also, remember that no matter what rewards you choose, you always need first to give yourself a hardy self-congratulations upon completing any action step, no matter how small.

❺ Upon completion of each step, cross the item off your list.

❻ At the end of the day, review your progress. This is an important step in the self-discipline process. If you got stuck on an action step, then you know that you need to take a look at whether Hyde had anything to do with it. Maybe you simply misjudged the time needed. But then again, maybe Hyde slipped in a roadblock on you. Daily reviews are a simple way to keep track of exactly what you actually do. Daily reviews will also keep you thinking about what you need to do to stay on the right path toward your goal, and help you get back on track when you falter. Sound easy? It is. After launch day, you will start making a short, simple daily "to do" list.

Important: The Preparation Stage requires that you use Visualization, Vitaminds, and Self-talk to psychologically prepare for action. Use these tools prior to action, on a daily basis. Put them to work for you as soon as you wake up; then use them many times during the day; then use them before drifting off to sleep. These simple tools are your friends. They will help you get whatever you want. They are a vital part of your self-discipline strategy.

17.

The
Action
Stage

Action Stage

Welcome to the Action Stage of the self-discipline process. But before you enter let's make sure you are prepared. Are you ready for action?

You need to know:

. . . the psychological information you learned during your ten day course. You do not need to know everything. But you need to know the basics so that you can use the tools and techniques that fit your personality, goals, and situation.

You need to know:

. . . how your personal Hyde works on you. Which tactics? When? Why? You will need this when faced with uninviting action steps.

You need to know:

. . . how to use all five tools. The more you use them, the more you will see your self-discipline efforts growing easier and easier. When Hyde pulls you away from self-discipline ask "What specifically am I telling myself that is making me resist doing this step?" Then wait for an answer, which will come from the poisons, fears, and self-defeating beliefs that you learned about in earlier chapters. When you get an answer you can then use your tools to counter Hyde's influence, and keep yourself motivated. Put Vitaminds all over the place. When you look at those Vitaminds use Relaxation for a minute and really take in those messages. Consciously use self-talk throughout the day, especially before sleeping and upon rising. During the day Visualize yourself completing your goal and savoring the payoff. Visualize for a minute, repeat frequently. Again, use your tools, it's easy and rewarding. Speaking of rewards: *Use them!*

You need to know:

. . . when Hyde is minimizing the effects of self-discipline break-downs, and justifying self-discipline roadblocks. You need to be ready with prepared responses to Hyde's attempts to sidetrack you.

What you need to do in the Action Stage:

❶ Make a simple daily "to do" list. For your first list you can use the one you made during the Preparation Stage. Here is what makes this list different from most: Next to each step write a guess at how many minutes you plan to work on the step, not prepare for, but actually do the step. When writing your steps, always keep them small.

Important: Remember that you are likely to *overestimate* the time needed for an unpleasant step, and *underestimate* the time needed for a pleasant step. The good news is that your uninviting steps will be over quicker than you imagined.

❷ Do one minute of relaxation before doing each step.

❸ Put a line through the step when completed.

❹ At the end of the day take a look at your list. Reward yourself, no matter how few steps toward your goal were completed. Small steps add up fast. So thank yourself and Hyde for each completed step, then remember to place each uncompleted step on tomorrow's "to do" list. If you carry the same step more than five days maybe you need to break that step into smaller steps. Or take a look at what you are telling yourself about that step that is making it difficult for you.

About time management:

Your conscious use of times and dates plays an important role in the self-discipline process, especially in the Action Stage. But don't maximize the importance of time management and minimize the importance of self-management. Without self-management no time management system will work for you. Besides, no one actually manages time. You can only manage yourself. The amount of time in hours, days, weeks, months, and years remains stable regardless of what you do or don't do. No matter how you plan your day, it will never be 29 hours long, only 24.

You can, however, direct your choices and behavior in a way that gives you more of what you want from each of the days, those 24 hour time blocks that you regularly receive. So think of clocks and calendars as friends, good buddies that provide you with friendly reminders. Do not think of clocks and calendars as enemies, evil faces hanging over your head like dark clouds of doom. Think "target date," not "*dead*line." You will receive a self-discipline boost when you see a written start time, and Hyde will be comforted by seeing a written stop time.

Important: Use all of your tools during the Action Stage. Change your Vitaminds regularly so you don't become so used to seeing them that they lose their impact. Some people find that changing them weekly works best. Other people change them every couple of weeks. The same goes for self-talk. Even after you find that certain tools work better than others, continue to use a variety of tools rather than finding one, such as self-talk, and sticking with only that one. Also, here is where your Rewards, big and small, will make a lot of difference. And whenever you have a difficult time getting yourself to do any of the steps toward your goal, go back and look over the psychological information that you received in the *Self-Discipline in 10 days* course. Also check your *Decision* and *Preparation* work. With a bit of brief detective work you will find out why you are stalling, and how you can overcome the problem.

Important: If you occasionally slip up during the Action Stage, do not get on your own case about it. This is a normal occurrence; something to be expected. Do not expect Perfection and berate yourself for not achieving it. Do the opposite; give yourself credit for at least trying. This approach to dealing with slip-ups will give you psychological encouragement to quickly get back into action. Self put-downs is one of Hyde's tricks. Don't fall for it!

Now, you are ready to go into action. The next stage, Maintenance and Completion, will show you ways to keep you going.

18.

The Completion / Maintenance Stage

Completion / Maintenance

When you reach this stage, you will have already completed a series of steps toward your chosen goal. Maybe you have already reached your goal and need to maintain it, such as when you have lost thirty pounds and need self-discipline to keep them off. Or, you may have actually completed your goal, such as owning a new auto.

But regardless of whether you need to maintain your goal or complete your goal, the requirements of this stage are Awareness, Attitude, and continued Action. Don't take this stage lightly. I want to emphasize that the Completion/Maintenance Stage is just as important as the Action Stage, and it requires just as much attention and effort. In fact, regained pounds after a successful diet is an example of action without maintenance. So is a cleaned out garage that gets junky again after six months.

Because you can easily become over-confident due to success with the Action Stage, you are now especially susceptible to Hyde's tricks. How does Hyde work against you during the Completion/Maintenance stage?

Hyde uses the same tricks that were used during the other stages. Except that during this stage Hyde also uses your success against you."I worked on that report all weekend, so I deserve a break tonight, right?" Or, "Heck, I haven't smoked for three weeks, why not have a few tonight?" Indeed, Hyde uses the good events *and* the bad events to block your self-discipline. "I'm so upset about Joe that I don't feel like even looking at that stupid report tonight" Or, "I'm so happy about the way things worked out with Joe that I'm going to celebrate tonight. I'll work on that report some other time."

In other words, Hyde tries to erode the commitment you made during the Decision Stage. So, suddenly, as you near completion of your project, Hyde brings up all the negative aspects of achieving your goal. Then, after having used self-discipline quite sucessfully during the Action Stage, you find yourself making excuses rather than continuing action. This is when you need to use *Awareness*, *Attitude*, and continued *Action*.

Awareness: Be alert! Don't let Hyde subconsciously use rationalization and justification to make you slack off on your self-discipline. Don't minimize the importance of each little step you need to take in order to get where you want to go. Use Relaxation to turn the volume up on Hyde's messages. Then you can find out *specifically* what you are telling yourself that blocks your progress. When you can hear Hyde's *specific* negative self-talk, you can counter and replace it with supportive messages.

Attitude: Your feelings play an important role in self-discipline. If you *feel* you can reach your goal, then you are already halfway there. During the Completion/Maintenance Stage, Hyde will try to short-circuit your attitude in many different ways. You can counter Hyde's influence on your attitude by using Self-talk, Visualization, and Vitaminds.

Action: You need to be aware of your consistency level during the Completion/Maintenance Stage, the same as you were during the Action Stage. People who have self-discipline difficulties tend to slack off as they get closer to the finish line. To guard against this tendency you need to pay close attention to your daily plan. Make sure you are actually *doing* things, not just *thinking* about them. In other words, monitor your progress daily, especially as you get closer to completion. Here you need to use Rewards more than ever.

So whether you need to complete a one-time project or maintain self-discipline in a specific area of your life for weeks, months, years, or a lifetime. You can do it by consciously using your knowledge and tools. If you run into self-discipline difficulty during the Completion/Maintenance Stage, try the following quick, easy exercise to get back into the self-discipline process.

❶ Pinpoint the *specific* action that you are not doing. If you are avoiding a series of actions, focus on the first one. You might find that all you need to do is break down this task into smaller, bite-size tasks. If not, go to step two.

❷ Ask yourself: "Why am I putting this task off?" "What *specific* poison, roadblock, or belief is Hyde using?" In other words, "What *specifically* am I telling myself about this *specific* action?" Be alert for rationalizations and justifications.

❸ What do you gain by putting it off? Uncover *specific payoffs*. Ask yourself: "Is it worth it?"

❹ What will you *lose* by putting it off? Be honest about your real *feelings*. Don't minimize the consequences.

❺ What wonderful benefits will you receive when you reach your goal? Use Visualization to really see your success. Use your emotions to really *feel* the pleasure of seeing yourself complete your goal.

Remember: If you have problems maintaining self-discipline at this stage, you probably didn't put enough time and effort into the first two self-discipline stages—the Decision Stage and the Preparation Stage.

Very Important: Personalize all you've learned. Experiment with all the tools and techniques to find out what works best for you. Do everything your way. And do remember to regularly alternate tools and techniques. When you use the same tools without variation they lose their energy. So if you fall into a pattern of relying on certain tools, at least vary their content. This means: Use different visualizations. Try new sentences with self-talk. Renew your Vitamind prescriptions with fresh, energizing phrases that help you focus.

Very, Very Important: Personalize Hyde. Friend or foe, Hyde will always be with you. So I suggest that you make the relationship a supportive one. With this in mind, I *strongly* suggest that you give *your* Hyde a friendly, personal name. Use this name during all conversations and negotiations with Hyde. Using a special name for Hyde reminds you instantly that *dealing with Hyde is like dealing with a person different from yourself.* Again, be sure to make the name friendly.

As a young child did you have a nickname, maybe a name that only your family called you? Your childhood nickname will work especially well because Hyde, psychologically speaking, is a reflection of the child *you* were. So always keep this in mind during conversations and negotiations with Hyde. Have you ever noticed how a salesperson calls you by name at every possible opportunity? They do this because it makes you more receptive to their proposition. When you deal with Hyde, *you* are the salesperson. You want to sell Hyde on the concept of maximum cooperation and minimum conflict. You want to sell the idea that if the task gets done, you both win. So take a tip from the sales world and always address Hyde by a personalized name. Believe me, you will be pleasantly surprised at how much this helps you with self-discipline.

A final note!

Remember: Self-discipline is a teachable and learnable process. Anyone who learns the process can apply it in any chosen situation. Self-discipline is not a personality trait, not "I *have* self-discipline." It is a skill, "I *use* self-discipline."

Using this skill, like using any other skill, grows easier with practice. And every time you use it, you're practicing. So regularly use what you've learned, occasionally refresh your knowledge, and enjoy your accomplishments!

Additional information

For information about self-discipline courses, workshops, seminars, articles, and speaking engagements contact:

> **Theodore Bryant, MSW**
> c/o HUB Publishing
> Box 15352
> Seattle, WA 98115

Also, you are cordially invited to share your self-discipline stories, tips, and techniques with Theodore Bryant by writing to the above address.

about the author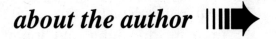

About the author . . .

Theodore Bryant, MSW

For over a decade, human behavior expert Theodore Bryant has conducted self-discipline courses, workshops, and seminars. He is the author of *Self-Discipline In 10 Days*.

His professional background includes experience as a Psychotherapist, a Gerontologist, a writer, and a speaker. He is a former clinical faculty member at the University of Utah Graduate School of Social Work. He has lectured at universities such as University of Washington, University of Tennessee at Chattanooga, University of Utah, and University of Oregon.

Mr. Bryant has developed numerous staff training videos, resource guides for consumers, and a variety of handbooks for local, state, and federal agencies, as well as for private businesses. He has served as a consultant on projects funded by diverse sources such as Seattle/King County Developmental Disabilities Division and Small Business Innovation Research, a federal program.

Through his many media appearances, Mr. Bryant has helped thousands of people develop and strengthen their self-discipline. His self-discipline courses have reached people from a wide range of fields—from artists to athletes, from business people to the general public. His dynamic teaching style has often been described as "painless and effective." Combining wit with wisdom, he keeps listeners laughing while learning *how to* increase their self-discipline—*fast!*

> "Theodore Bryant, MSW, has created an exciting, powerful, and extremely effective self-discipline course. His 'crash' course will take you from thinking, dreaming, and hoping to doing!"
>
> *Hub Publishing*